"Years of over-dependence on political activism has left most Christians timid to engage in the political process. Now, more than ever, we need a positive, proactive vision for how to live out the gospel to the public square. Ashford and Pappalardo give us a masterfully constructed blueprint for doing so."

J. D. Greear, pastor of The Summit Church, Raleigh-Durham, North Carolina, and author of *Gaining by Losing: Why the Future Belongs to Churches that Send*

"During my time as an evangelical pastor, I urged my congregation to take their faith seriously and to live lives of moral clarity. Then, during the more than a decade I spent as Governor of Arkansas, my leadership aim was the same—to provide moral clarity, character, and conviction. This impressive book invites Christians to approach politics with both courage and compassion, in the hope that we can once again call ourselves one nation, under God. Most importantly, it offers something that's in short supply in politics these days—hope."

Mike Huckabee, former governor of Arkansas, Baptist pastor, bestselling author, candidate for U.S. President

"Again and again I nodded my head with a hearty 'yes' to Ashford and Pappalardo's vision of Christian political engagement. And in those places I would have expected to shake my head 'no,' they challenged me to stop and rethink. Anyone interested in the topic should read this book."

Jonathan Leeman, editorial director of 9Marks and author of *Political Church: The Local Assembly as Embassy of Christ's Rule*

"*One Nation Under God* is a thoughtful, readable primer on Christian political engagement. This book is rooted firmly in biblical authority and gospel depth. Anyone seeking to make sense out of the Christian's place in the civic order will benefit."

Russell Moore, president, Southern Baptist Ethics & Religious Liberty Commission

"In this highly readable and insightful book, Bruce Ashford and Chris Pappalardo offer wisdom for all of us who know that all that we do—in public and in private—takes place "under God." And we can be thankful that they go beyond generalities to speak in helpful and practical ways to some of the pressing issues that require much Christian discernment these days!"

Richard J. Mouw, president emeritus and professor of faith and public life, Fuller Theological Seminary

"What does faithful Christian political witness look like in post-Christian America? Ashford and Pappalardo provide a sound, sober, and gospel-guided answer, which is exactly what we need today."

R. R. Reno, editor, *First Things*

ONE NATION UNDER GOD

ONE NATION UNDER GOD

A Christian Hope for American Politics

BRUCE ASHFORD AND CHRIS PAPPALARDO

ACADEMIC

Nashville, Tennessee

978-1-4336-9069-3

Published by B&H Publishing Group
Nashville, Tennessee

Dewey Decimal Classification: 261.7
Subject Heading: CHRISTIANITY AND POLITICS \ CHURCH
AND STATE \ POLITICS

1 2 3 4 5 6 7 8 • 20 19 18 17 16 15

To my parents, Bruce and Bobbi Ashford, and
my parents-in-law, Joe and Dana Sanders.
—Bruce Riley Ashford

To my wife, Jennifer, who continues to teach me
what it means to fix my eyes on things unseen.
—Chris Pappalardo

Contents

Acknowledgments

We wish to thank Chris Thompson and Jim Baird at B&H Academic for their commitment to this project and the excellence with which they carried out their editorial roles. We are thankful for Jackie Sanderlin and Cindy Hotchkiss, who assisted in preparing the manuscript for submission. We also wish to thank those who provided expert feedback on various portions of the manuscript, including Richard Mouw, Jonathan Leeman, Erik Clary, Andrew Walker, Andrew Spencer, Walter Strickland, Barrett Duke, and Daniel Heimbach.

I (Bruce) am grateful for friends and colleagues from whom I have learned much about Christianity, politics, and the public square. I think of Daniel Heimbach, David Jones, and Mark Liederbach at Southeastern Baptist Theological Seminary; Stephen Grabill at Acton Institute; Russell Moore at the Ethics and Religious Liberty Commission; and R. Albert Mohler at The Southern Baptist Theological Seminary. I am grateful also for public theologians from whose biographies and writings I have benefitted over the years, including Abraham Kuyper, Richard John Neuhaus, Martin Luther King Jr., and Lesslie Newbigin. Among contemporary public theologians, I am especially indebted to Richard Mouw, whose writings have helped me understand what public faithfulness might look like in an increasingly plural and post-Christian America.

I (Chris) am grateful for the many mentors and friends who have helped show me how inherently public Christianity is. Chief among them is Bruce Ashford, without whom I might never have encountered the rich world of thought represented by men like Richard John Neuhaus. Nor would the books of Lesslie Newbigin have entered my library if it had not been for the dogged persistence of Thomas West. I think appreciatively of J. D. Greear, who has not only taught me to read Scripture deeply but has also equipped me to express biblical truth incisively and to apply it broadly. And I wish to thank the many men and women who have graciously indulged me in conversations spanning the entire subject matter of this book. Your influence is throughout (and I owe you each at least a lunch). Finally, I am grateful for the many unnamed Americans who, though knowing nothing of Neuhaus, Newbigin, or Kuyper, already live out the precepts in this little book, simply by faithfully following Jesus.

Introduction

G. K. Chesterton once noted, "Seemingly from the dawn of man all nations have had governments, and all nations have been ashamed of them."[1] What is true of "all nations" is often particularly true for Christians. When we stop to consider government and politics, our hearts are not strangely warmed but rather filled with apprehension and angst. Politics may be necessary in today's world, but many of us are inclined to think of it as a necessary *evil*.

Not all Christians, however, are so down on politics. In fact, over the past few decades, many evangelicals have remained markedly active in the political realm even while effectively retreating from other aspects of public culture—most notably the arts, entertainment, and science. We evangelicals have never stopped wanting to change our country, but we've too often voluntarily limited ourselves to one tool: the hammer of political activism. And when the only tool you have is a hammer, every problem begins to look like a nail.[2]

Thus some Christians think of politics as an insufferable necessity; others conceive of politics as nigh unto salvation. Ironically, these two perspectives tend to feed off each other. Those who imbue politics with unrealistic and salvific expectations are most liable to conclude—even if it takes years to get there—that politics is not worth it after all and must be abandoned at all costs. "Politics as salvation" leads to political

1

frustration, which leads to political withdrawal. For many well-intentioned believers, what begins as an arena of endless hope often ends as an arena of darkness and despair.

The lives of nationally syndicated columnist Cal Thomas and pastor Ed Dodson show this unfortunate progression. In 1999, after thirty years of conservative political activism with the Moral Majority, they counseled evangelicals to give up activism entirely.[3] Politics, they said, was too corrupt an arena for Christians to use to enact social change. Best to stick to the work of saving souls.

We understand the frustration of men like Thomas and Dodson. Politics has been a rocky shoal on which countless hopes have been shipwrecked. But still we maintain in no uncertain terms: withdrawal is not an option.

If we are not to withdraw from politics, is it possible to avoid the opposite error of making politics our sole tool for societal change? How can we navigate between the dual extremes of political withdrawal and political salvation? Can we really engage in politics responsibly, confidently, graciously—in a word, *Christianly*?

These are the questions that drive this little book. And they are questions of special significance at the beginning of the twenty-first century, as the United States is quickly becoming a post-Christian country. For the first time in the history of our country, Christians are often considered morally inferior or even evil because they embrace historic Christian teaching. This situation has evoked responses of both activism and withdrawal. And it has created an atmosphere of intense emotion. Some Christians are fearful. Others are angry. Most are confused, wanting to rightly relate their Christianity to politics and public life but not knowing *how*.

That is the purpose of this book. We hope to share a perspective on politics that tempers the expectations of those with inflated hopes, empowers those with deflated hopes, and equips every Christian to apply Christ's love in the muddied arena of politics. Politics is not an evil arena to be avoided. Neither is it our only avenue for impacting society. The reality is much more complex and, oddly enough, much more promising.

In the first chapter we show that the Bible's "big story" provides the context within which Christians should think about politics and public life. Only by considering the four plot movements of Scripture—creation, fall, redemption, and restoration—can we begin to understand the role of politics today. In chapter 2 we identify four competing answers to the question of Christianity and politics, digging a bit deeper to show that each answer actually rests on a unique understanding of grace. In the third chapter we show how Christianity is able to affect every sphere of life without creating a theocracy. Chapter 4 picks up the question of church and state specifically, asking—and answering—how our view of cultural engagement will affect our view of church-government relations.

In the fifth chapter we talk about the specific challenges of our cultural context. Contemporary Americans live in a country that is decreasingly Christian. While many Christians feel this as a threat, we argue that it is time for us to learn afresh how to witness to our society as a minority group, to minister from the margins. We must once again become comfortable as resident aliens in our own nation while still pursuing the welfare of our society. In the sixth chapter we provide practical advice on how to leverage public-square interactions as witness for Christ. Our political interaction is an avenue for proclaiming aspects of the gospel, for showing the world a different hope, and for displaying Christian character and discernment.

The next seven chapters address current topics in American politics—abortion, euthanasia, immigration, same-sex marriage, the economy, the environment, race relations, immigration, and just war. In these chapters we show how our view of Christianity and politics (addressed in chapters 1–6) applies in real life. Each chapter focuses on a Christian who has proven to be an exemplary public witness on the topic at hand.

In the final chapter we conclude by highlighting one last exemplary Christian, a hero from the past—Augustine of Hippo. Augustine lived during the decline of the Roman Empire and stood as a champion for Christianity when society had begun to decry the faith. We will summarize his famous book, *City of God*, which was written to address Rome's political ills, and apply its lessons to our own—surprisingly similar—American context.

Chapter 1

Locating Politics Within the True Story of the Whole World

When we ask the question, "How can we engage in politics as Christians?" it can be tempting to immediately jump to specific topics. That is, of course, how the conversation generally comes to us. *"What do you think about immigration?" "How should Christians approach abortion legislation?" "Which candidate are you voting for and why?"* But if we start answering each question without setting up a broader framework for politics, we are bound only to isolate or confuse.

The only way to overcome our fragmented perspective on contemporary politics is to allow a master narrative to shape the current conversation. As Richard John Neuhaus wrote, "The first thing to be said about public life is that public life is not the first thing."[1] Of course, party platforms and specific issues of public policy *do* matter. But policies shouldn't be crafted, and platforms shouldn't be constructed in ways that are divorced from the bigger picture. So we've got to go back before we can go forward. We need to locate politics within the true story of the whole world.

Act 1: Creation (Or: *Why Is There Something Rather Than Nothing?*)

"In the beginning, God created the heavens and the earth" (Gen 1:1). The Bible begins with the bald fact of God in action, and its first assertion immediately demands that the reader reorient himself to this truth. The world we see around us did not come to be as a result of atomic randomness. It is the intentional handiwork of a Being so supreme, so foundational, so high above our conception, that his first spoken word can rightly be called *the beginning*. Before he spoke, there was nothing. But after his first word, everything.

Evangelicals too often give insufficient thought to the doctrine of creation. We admit, of course, that God created everything and that he deemed the entire created order "good." But beyond that we struggle to find much relevance in creation.

So, what should we see in God's creative activity? For one, we should see the pinnacle of God's act of creation, his unique creation of humanity: *"Let us make man in our image, after our likeness"* (Gen 1:26). Humanity stands not merely as the crown of creation but as a radically *different* type of creation. God makes the animals "after their kind," but he crafts humans in *his* image and likeness. All of creation shows us something of God, but humanity has the distinct honor and privilege of bearing his image.

As God's image bearers, we are uniquely fitted to act on his behalf. The world we see around us is not our own, of course: "The earth is the LORD's and the fullness thereof, the world and those who dwell therein" (Ps 24:1). But God has chosen to govern his creation through intermediaries—through *us*. We steward God's creation because he has given us the reins. This is an awesome responsibility and an inescapable one. The same authoritative voice that effortlessly tossed stars into the night sky also boldly declared, "Let the sons of Adam and daughters of Eve have dominion over this creation" (Cf. Gen 1:28).

One of the ways humanity is meant to exercise God's loving dominion is through bringing out the latent potentials of God's created order, what is often called "culture work." Culture work entails cultivating the earth to produce food, cultivating relationships to produce flourishing families, cultivating legal systems to create order and peace, and cultivating financial systems to produce justice and equity. Whenever God's image bearers work to bring out the hidden potentials of God's creation, we are fulfilling God's plan for humanity, "tilling the earth" so that it might bear fruit.

The creation story shows us that the physical and earthly nature of culture does not make this work inferior to more "spiritual" matters. As Al Wolters says:

> God does not make junk, and we dishonor the Creator if
> we take a negative view of the work of his hands when he
> himself takes such a positive view. In fact, so positive a view
> did God take of what he had created that he refused to scrap
> it when mankind spoiled it, but determined instead, at the
> cost of his Son's life, to make it new and good again. *God
> does not make junk, and he does not junk what he has made.*[2]

One significant sphere of culture is politics. Because God commanded humanity to be fruitful and multiply, we know he intended the human race to grow, and anytime humans exist together in community, there is the need for government of some type. Before the fall, government would have consisted of some sort of collective ordering of human life—setting schedules, making policies, and so forth. For example, whether or not to drive on the right or left side of the road— even unfallen humans would have had to decide this. But because of the fall, as we will learn in a moment, government would have to expand to include the sword of Romans 13.

Although we might be tempted to view politics as something not worth our time or beyond the pale of God's power, we need to remind ourselves that God created the type of world in which a collective ordering of society is necessary, and he remains sovereign over this world. He is sovereign over politics and, to the extent that we find ourselves involved in public life, we should consciously allow him to be sovereign over our involvement.

Act 2: The Fall (Or: *Where Did We Go Wrong?*)

In the beginning there was peace. In the beginning there was love. God made Adam and Eve, gently placed them in the center of a beautiful and rustic world, and charged them to be fruitful, to till the soil, and to manage his good world. Later biblical teaching makes clear that these types of obedience are ways of loving God, one another, and the world. Created in love, humanity was to respond in love.

Sadly we chose another path. Our world was still in its infancy when our first parents turned from the source of all love, from love himself. We no longer loved God, one another, or our world. In place of love, hatred emerged. In place of peace, strife arose. Instead of justice reigning, injustice gained a foothold. And from the moment Adam and Eve plucked the forbidden fruit, we have all been suffering the poisonous effects of sin.

Adam and Eve's tragic rebellion led to death and brokenness in four dimensions. First, they experienced brokenness in their relationship with God. Rather than enjoying communion with God as their ultimate source of happiness and goodness, they became his enemies. God's presence, previously a joy, had become a terror.

Second, they experienced brokenness in their relationship with others. The fall initiated a world of which we are all too familiar, one filled with interpersonal evil. The serpent had promised to give humanity true life, but what we received instead was death in a thousand forms—murder, rape, divorce, adultery, slavery, terrorism, and genocide.

Third, they experienced brokenness in their relationship within themselves. By choosing to look inward as our source of authority instead of upward to God, we began a devastating trajectory. The wide and wondrous world in front of us shrunk down until it was only about us. As Martin Luther would say, humanity became *incurvatus se,* curved in on himself.[3] And a world consumed with personal desire is a world of everlasting longings and everlasting disappointments. We are not strong enough to carry our own soul.

Lastly, Adam and Eve precipitated brokenness in their relationship with the created order. No longer would they live in a paradise marked by universal flourishing and delight. Their fall dragged the entire created order into a horrifying downward spiral. As Wolters summarizes, this "was not just an isolated act of disobedience but an event of catastrophic significance for creation as a whole."[4] Adam and Eve's rebellion marked a turning point in history as not only humanity but all of creation plummeted into darkness and chaos. Politics and public life received a strong dose of sin's poison that day.

In the general sense of the word, *politics* is "the theory and practice of influencing other people in our society." In its more specific sense, *politics* refers to the governance of a society. So the political realm has everything to do with our relationships to other people. In the aftermath of the fall, the political realm remains *structurally* good but has been corrupted *directionally.*[5] In other words, God structured the world in such a way that we would have politics and public life, and the fact of its existence is good. But because of the depravity of the human heart, politics and public life are always to some extent directed toward idols rather than toward God.

This misdirection can be seen in the fact that God's imagers govern the world imperfectly, often in ways that are unjust, unwise, and unloving. Instead of viewing government as a realm in which we may wisely steward resources, far too often we grasp for power and trample the weak. Instead of using our public voice to bless and enrich others, we spew vitriol and create factions.

The problem runs deep, deeper than most political analysts even conceive. But the problem is never *politics*, per se. Liberals aren't the problem. Conservatives aren't the problem. Politicians aren't the problem. We are. We all are—because we all have the entrenched tendency to twist God's created order into idolatry. Pointed toward Christ, anything in creation becomes a blessing. Pointed away from him, the greatest blessing becomes a curse.[6]

Act 3: Redemption (Or: *Is There Hope for This World?*)

Only the most naïvely optimistic among us need reminders that our present world is in a horrible state. But the question remains: is there any hope? All the contemporary talk of being on the "wrong side of history" assumes that history is pointed toward something better than the past. But do we have any guarantee of that? Have our technological developments led to greater peace? Do our new ideologies protect the weak any better than the old ones? Is it not more obviously the case that the world is, and always will be, defined by increasingly creative means of brutality? As Alfred Lord Tennyson wrote, "Nature, red in tooth and claw . . . shriek[s] against [God's] creed."[7]

Our modern world desires hope and often looks to the future for better days. But apart from the gospel, Tennyson's dismal conclusion is the only appropriate one. Thankfully, Christians have a firm hope, based not in a wistful optimism but in history itself.

Humanity's descent into sin was quick, but the wonder of our God is that his plan of redemption began immediately. Bundled together with the consequences and curses of sin, God promised to destroy the serpent and undo the curse of sin (Gen 3:15; Gal 4:4–5). He would not allow his good creation to languish in brokenness but initiated his program of redemption and restoration even before we understood the depth of our fall. God promised that the alienation we now know—alienation from God, from others, from ourselves, from creation—would not have the final say.

What was a promise to Adam and Eve is a historical fact for us. God *did* come to earth in the person of Jesus Christ, proving how far he would come to recover his own. And Jesus *did* preach of a new kingdom, one in which God's peace, love, and flourishing would be restored. He *did* die on a cross as the sacrificial substitute for sinful humanity. He *did* step out of the grave three days later, forever settling the question of which kingdom will prevail.

The death and resurrection of Jesus Christ stand at the blazing center of God's redemptive acts in our world. In his death Jesus paid the costly price for sin that every one of us owed, and he did so with joy. He received the shame and punishment of our sin so that we might receive the joy and life of his righteousness. No Christian who has tasted of this *great exchange* comes away unchanged. It is a truth so profound, so overwhelming, that we can only reply: "Amazing grace, how sweet the sound, that saved a wretch like me!"[8]

The redemption that Christ brings holds immense value for the individual soul. But it does not end there. The scope of God's salvation is as broad as his creation (Rom 8:19–22). Thus while every political decision and action is tainted by the power of sin and death, another power is also at work. And at every moment when the power of death is at work seeking to claim every square inch of this universe, God's power—the power that raised his Son from the dead—is also at work, counter-claiming all of those inches.

Act 4: Restoration (Or: *What Does the Future Hold?*)

To an uninformed eyewitness observer, the events of Jesus Christ's execution would most likely have signaled a defeat. Here was an idealist martyr for a worthy cause but a martyr nonetheless. Jesus' death would have seemed tragic but almost inevitable. This is, after all, the way of the world. Who among us hasn't known the pain of seeing a beautiful and good pursuit end in tragedy? Even our greatest accomplishments contain within them the seeds of their own destruction. History's mill grinds slowly but, in the end, exceedingly fine. The dust heap of history ultimately claims it all.

So our experience teaches us that the natural end of every story is death. But the resurrection of Christ teaches us that this "ending" is penultimate. A new power has invaded this dying world, one that will renew and restore it. The resurrection stands not merely as a confirmation of Christ's divinity, nor even just as a foreshadowing of our bodily resurrections but also as a promise of future cosmic resurrection (Rev 21–22). When Christ left his tomb behind him, he uttered history's decisive victory cry. The wonder of it all is that we are privy to this finale *before the finale.* We have seen a glimpse of the end, and yet we live in the middle of the script.

God will restore the earth, and his kingdom will prevail. What he created, what he mourned over as it rebelled against him, what he pursued and redeemed—*this* he will restore from top to bottom. The Father does not intend to trash his creation and pluck us up out of it. He will do for creation what he did for his Son. He will take the dead and make it alive, more alive than ever before.

As those who know the end of history's story, Christians can engage in political activity with an unabashed confidence. The political realm, as dark as it may often seem, will one day be raised to life, made to bow in submission to Christ. But our role in God's kingdom remains that of *witnesses,* so our boldness is prevented from becoming triumphalism. Christ will gain victory and restore the earth, but it will be *his* victory.

Lesslie Newbigin, a twentieth-century missionary theologian, recognized the profound implications that history's final act had for contemporary social action. With the new heavens and new earth in our sights, we are imbued with both humility and boldness in our daily faithfulness: humility because our best efforts will always end in decay, boldness because God will not let them languish there. We can provide no more fitting conclusion to this chapter than Newbigin's words:

> The point is that [a transformed society] is not our goal, great as that is. . . . Our goal is the holy city, the New Jerusalem, a perfect fellowship in which God reigns in every heart, and His children rejoice together in His love and joy. . . . And though we know that we must grow old and die, that *our labors, even if they succeed for a time, will in the end be buried in the dust of time,* and that along with the painfully won achievements of goodness, there are mounting seemingly irresistible forces of evil, *yet we are not dismayed.* . . . We know that these things must be. But we know that as surely as Christ was raised from the dead, so surely shall there be a new heaven and a new earth wherein dwells righteousness. *And having this knowledge we ought as Christians to be the strength of every good movement of political and social effort, because we have no need either of blind optimism or of despair.*[9]

Chapter 2

Choosing Between Four Competing Views of Public Life

Russian winters are not known for affording a cornucopia of options for how to spend one's evenings. When the temperature regularly drops to ten or twenty below zero for months at a time, there is little to do. So when I (Bruce) found myself in Russia during the winters of 1998 and 1999, I had a lot of time on my hands. And that is when I first had the time and motivation to reflect on the different views Christians have about politics.

My years in Russia provided the perfect context for reflecting on Christianity, politics, and the public square—for two reasons. First, evangelical Christian influence in Russia had been restricted severely during the Soviet era. Because I worked as an adjunctive professor at several universities in the city of Kazan, I rubbed elbows with Russian students and faculty members regularly. Most of them were deeply skeptical about whether God existed, whether life had any meaning, and whether there were any moral absolutes. Russia's cultural institutions—including its government, businesses, marriages, and schools—reflected this deep sense of loss.

Second, I compared and contrasted the Russian situation with my American context. I expected to see strong differences. But other than obvious surface-level variances, what struck me was the deep *similarity* between the two. Although Americans had never experienced a Soviet-style oppression of evangelical Christianity, the United States was becoming increasingly post-Christian. I had recently graduated from college, an environment in which many American students and faculty harbored the same skepticism about God, life, and meaning. I saw that our cultural institutions, too, were beginning to reflect the same deep sense of loss.

I certainly didn't enjoy the brutal cold at the time, but in retrospect I am grateful for those long Russian winters. Without them I would not have had time to reflect in a sustained manner on the various approaches Christians have taken to politics and public life. I might never have discovered the theological framework I needed for understanding a Christian's relationship to society and culture. I might have blithely continued to think of the United States as a "Christian nation," falling into one of the two all-too-common ditches of political engagement. I would have given politics too much weight or none at all.

Looking back, I now realize that I was just discovering what theologians call the "nature-grace" relationship. This nature-grace relationship is the deep structure underlying any view of Christianity and public life. Thus when one Christian says that politics is a waste of time, he does so not because of *politics* but because of what he believes about *nature* and *grace*. So, what are nature and grace? By *nature* we mean the created world we live in, along with the spheres of culture that find their home in the created realm. By *grace* we refer to God's gracious salvation. And when another Christian throws all of her energy into political activism, again, her activity says more about her view of grace and nature, about the relationship of our salvation to our earthly life, than about politics per se.

So, how do nature and grace relate? Over the centuries various Christian answers have been given to this question, of which we will mention four. Each answer draws from the four acts of Scripture we have already outlined—creation, fall, redemption, restoration. Where they differ is in discerning the *meaning* of each act, the *relationship* between those acts, and the relative *importance* of each act. In many ways the answer to this question shapes the entirety of a person's worldview, theology, and spirituality. It influences one's view of theology and culture, Christianity and politics, and church and state.[1]

Now, before we outline these views, it bears mentioning that while we consider some more faulty than others, each camp has proponents that represent its view *well* and others that represent it *poorly*. The healthiest members of any category will, in many ways, look more like one another than the other members of the category we have created for them. Thus, while adjudicating among these views, it is helpful to see those of other views not as opponents but as fellow travelers toward right belief and practice.

Grace Against Nature: A Plague on the Political House

During my earliest years as a Christian, I (Bruce) held a view which can be called *grace against nature*. Although I would not have known to use the phrase, that was my view. The core conviction of this view is that the fall has corrupted the natural world *ontologically*—in its very being. Sin destroyed the goodness of God's creation such that it cannot be redeemed. So God will one day graciously destroy it and start over again. Instead of making all things new, he will make all new things. Historically, this view has been associated, and sometimes unfairly, with Anabaptists and monastics.

This vision promotes a distinctive way of life. Since the world is corrupted in its very being, it is not our home. A good Christian should, therefore, withdraw from the evil world and seek a salvation separate from it. The application to politics is rather obvious: while Christian citizens might speak prophetically against the powers in the political realm, they will hardly try to transform it or use it to achieve godly ends. Political action and public square involvement cannot be counted as "kingdom work" or considered part of the "Christian mission."

This vision has significant strengths, the greatest of which is that it takes sin seriously. Proponents of this view recognize the twisting and corrupting power of sin and speak prophetically against its manifestations in society and culture. Nature is, indeed, in desperate need of grace.

But separating nature and grace in this manner does not, in our view, comport with the biblical testimony. First and foremost, while it is wise to take sin seriously, this view gives sin far *too much* credit. Nature has been corrupted but not to the point of being *ontologically* or essentially bad. Satan simply isn't that powerful: he cannot make God's good world patently evil. His power is always derivative: he can only warp and poison. But that which is warped and poisoned remains structurally good.

Additionally, this view unintentionally undermines Christ's universal lordship, in effect limiting his reign to the realm of the church and the individual soul. But the Bible never paints a picture of a teeny, tiny Jesus who hides in our heart with an individualized gospel. It portrays a Jesus whose lordship is as wide as creation, whose kingly reign extends to every sphere of cultural life—including the political ones. When we display his lordship, regardless of the venue, we follow Jesus in Christian mission.

Lastly, proponents of this view might find themselves trapped. Because they consider nature so corrupt, they attempt to escape culture. But as humans who are part of the created order and whom God created as thoroughly cultural beings, we can no more escape these cultural realities than we can jump out of our own skin. The Christian life is, for good or for ill, an inherently cultural and political life.

Grace Above Nature: Bottom-Floor Politics

Even when I was a proponent of the *grace against nature* position, it made me a bit uncomfortable. I wanted a way to make sense of art, science, politics, and other parts of life that were not patently religious. How did Christ's lordship apply to these areas? I wanted to understand how Christians could bring the Christian faith to bear on those dimensions of life. After all, it was these dimensions—not church attendance or private devotions—that make up the majority of a person's waking hours. But I couldn't see how.

During those years I began to read books written by Christian thinkers whose vision could be characterized as one of *grace above nature*. This vision relates grace and nature hierarchically. In this view the Christian divides his time between the upper and lower realms. In the upper realm (grace), he has personal devotions, church attendance, and theology. In the lower realm (nature), he has a family, a workplace, a community, and certain leisure activities. The upper story is more important than the lower story, but it's also more damaged by sin. So God's grace and his special revelation are needed to fix the upper realm, whereas different tools are needed—less obviously religious ones—to fix the lower realm. Historically this view has been associated with certain versions of Thomism in both Roman Catholicism and Protestantism.

Politics and public life are, as you may imagine, part of that lower story. Because God's grace and special revelation are not needed in the lower story, Christians should usually refrain from employing them in their political activities. They can participate in politics but should rely on their consciences, reasoning abilities, political precedent, and other tools common to all humanity. God's grace and special revelation are for the upper realm—where they are desperately needed. But they do not need to be brought into the lower realm. Think of special revelation and politics as you think of cooking: keep your slotted spoon and chef's knife in the kitchen; don't bring them down to the basement.

This view has certain strengths. Unlike the *grace against nature* vision, it does not give sin too much credit. It rightly recognizes that sin cannot ontologically corrupt what God has made inherently good. But it swings too far in the other direction, failing to recognize the misdirecting power of sin in the natural realm and the necessity of bringing God's grace to bear in that realm in order to redirect it toward God. After all, if the roof is leaking, the whole house will have water damage, not just the upper story.

In short, this view does not recognize sufficiently that we must *always* draw upon biblical teaching when formulating our political views, even if we do not always draw upon it when articulating those views.

Grace Alongside Nature: Politicians and Pastors, Dual Ministers of God

A third theological framework is one we can call the *grace alongside nature* vision. In this view God's world is divided into two kingdoms, both of which he alone rules—a natural kingdom and a spiritual kingdom.[2] God rules the *natural* kingdom as Creator and Sustainer and does so through common grace and general revelation. He rules the *spiritual* kingdom as Redeemer and does so through saving grace and special revelation. This kingdom is already manifested in the life and ministry of the church. Historically this view has been associated with Luther and Lutherans but more recently and increasingly is associated with certain Reformed and Presbyterians theologians who draw heavily on Luther.

Proponents of this vision conceive of the two kingdoms as running on parallel tracks. They may be held in tension with each other but should never be conflated. A Christian operating in the natural realm should not, as Luther once put it, "drag [Christ's] words into the law books or into the secular government. . . . With the secular area [Christ] has nothing to do."[3] The natural realm (kingdom) has its own integrity. The church has its own integrity. The two exist side by side.

Proponents of the *grace alongside nature* vision can sound a lot like the *grace above nature* camp. They encourage us not to spiritualize the natural realm by pursuing cultural activities in the hope that we can transform the world, change the culture, or bring healing to the natural realm. Healing and transformation—these can only come through the gospel. Although our work in the natural realm has real value, it cannot rightly be part of Christian mission.

But if *grace above nature* tends to imply that grace is the more important realm (grace is, after all, the *higher* realm), the *grace alongside nature* position does not, or at least not as much. The two realms are distinct; yet they are of similar value. The pastor applies a supernaturally revealed gospel, while the politician applies his naturally gifted reason, but both men are agents of God. And both are engaged in godly endeavors and callings.

Yet the nature of the separation between the two realms remains problematic. For instance, politics in this view strives to formulate public convictions without appeal to special revelation. The gospel is out of bounds in the political arena. Just as in the *grace above nature* vision, this view tends to keep nature and grace in airtight compartments. God rules his church through Jesus; and while he rules politics, too, we needn't "bring Jesus into" our politics. Nor should we consider our political involvement "kingdom work" or "Christian mission."

This vision has great strengths, correcting some of the oversights of the previous two views. It takes both nature and grace seriously on their own merits, acknowledging that different settings require different applications of God's rule. But many of the same problems that plague *grace above nature* are evident throughout *grace alongside nature.* By limiting the usefulness of special revelation in the natural realm, this view fails to recognize how deeply sin has corrupted that realm. We agree that God gives to all human beings the ability to reason about social, cultural, moral, and political matters and that we should draw upon such general revelation when speaking about matters of public life in the public square. However, all people's hearts are shot through with sin and idolatry; they need God's special revelation to help them recognize general revelation and interpret it correctly. In other words, we still need the Bible to inform what happens in the political arena.

Most important, if God's special revelation is not put to work in the natural realm, then other gods will fill the vacuum. All social and cultural actions are underlain by some sort of religious vantage point, and if the church forsakes its own religious vantage point, it has no place to stand when critiquing other viewpoints. In other words, even though the grace alongside nature view was meant to empower cultural engagement, it has often fostered an unhealthy cultural and political passivity.[4]

Grace Renews Nature: A Political Preview of a Coming Kingdom

In the fourth and final vision, *grace renews nature*. In this vision grace is not opposed to the natural realm, but neither does it hover above the natural realm or live in tension alongside the natural realm. Instead, grace restores the natural realm but also renews it, making the natural realm even better than it was before the fall. Historically this view is associated with Abraham Kuyper and Herman Bavinck and finds support among contemporary theologians such as John Frame, Craig Bartholomew, and N. T. Wright.

Proponents of this view emphasize that God called creation (nature) into existence and ordered it by means of his word. His ordering word still holds for all of our life in the creational—or natural—realm. But another competing word is at work in the world, a word that threatens the natural realm. If God's creative and ordering word is his *thesis* for the world, sin is the *antithesis* to that thesis. The natural realm is marked by a conflict between the two.

We can see this thesis-antithesis struggle in the biblical plot line itself. At creation God instructed his imagers to be fruitful and multiply (a social command), till the soil (a cultural command), and have dominion over creation (a kingly command). After the fall his imagers continued to live as social, cultural, and political beings, but their actions and interactions were shot through with sin and idolatry. As a result, all of their doings were warped and misdirected. Sadly, therefore, we never had the chance to see what untainted social and cultural life—including politics—would have been like.

Indeed, instead of trusting the word God has spoken (his *thesis*), Adam and Eve believed and trusted the word of the serpent—history's first *antithesis*. And since that fateful day, all of humanity has lived in the tension between God's *thesis* and Satan's ever-present *antithesis*. This *antithesis* takes many forms but is any word spoken against God's word, any misdirection of the natural world as God intended it. To use the terms we introduced in the previous chapter, nature remains *structurally* good, but our sin consistently corrupts it *directionally*. The raw materials have been poisoned and pointed toward idols, but the materials themselves remain good.

God's response to Satan's *antithesis* was not a fresh reset but a promise of renewal. Nature had become sick, and grace was the cure. The body of creation had been shot through with poison—a poison extending to every sphere of human life, a poison running to our very core, a poison unto death. But God sent his Son as an antidote to absorb sin's curse and heal nature's body. Christ's death and resurrection promise that he will one day liberate creation from its bondage, purifying creation of every corruption and misdirection (Rom 8:19–22; Rev 21:1).

This is salvation: purification, renewal, liberation, restoration, healing, and reconciliation. None of these terms implies a clean sweep, a replacement of one "bad" world with a newer and better one. The salvation God brings into this world transforms it from the inside out. God's grace is not *against* nature. It does not float *above* nature. And it does not merely exist *alongside* it. God's grace renews and restores nature, making it what he always intended it to be.

The Dutch theologian Abraham Kuyper described this renewal well:

> For if grace exclusively concerned atonement for sin and
> salvation of souls, one could view grace as something located
> and operating outside of nature. . . . But if it is true that
> Christ our Savior has to do not only with our soul but also
> with our body . . . then of course everything is different.
> We see immediately that *grace* is inseparably connected with
> *nature*, that grace and nature belong together.[5]

Living in a fallen world, it may seem to us that God's grace is incompatible with the natural realm, but we must remind ourselves that the incompatibility is directional rather than structural and that all things will be redirected toward Christ in the end.

This means that we as believers must be *redirective* in our social, cultural—and, yes, political—activities. We seek to have God's incarnate and written word shape our words and actions. We inquire about God's creational *thesis* for politics and public life, discern the many ways sin speaks an *antithesis* to this design, and find ways to redirect politics toward Christ. This is an act of love for our neighbors, an act of obedience toward our King, and an act of eschatological hope. By faithfully redirecting the political realm, we paint a preview of Christ's coming kingdom, when he will renew this heavens and earth.

If we are able actually to transform culture, improving it through our political preview, then so be it. But that is not the ultimate goal. Any cultural transformation we see will be neither comprehensive nor enduring. It will, either quickly or slowly, fall on the dust heap of history, seemingly lost forever. If we aim to win a culture war, we will likely only be disappointed and disillusioned.

But if we trust the victory Christ has promised—that he has, indeed, already accomplished at Calvary—then our feeble acts of faithfulness will be resurrected. What we preview for the world today will become reality on that last day. Redemption will finally transform us in the totality of our being, across the entire fabric of our lives.

We live in the midst of a cosmic struggle, and while the outcome is certain, Christ's kingship is not universally acknowledged *today*. As C. S. Lewis once said, "There is no neutral ground in the universe. Every square inch, every split second is claimed by God, and counter-claimed by Satan."[6] Thus every act of obedience—including political obedience—is a part of Christian mission, a bold declaration that we support God's claim to the throne. And because the assault on that throne comes from every nook and cranny of creation, we must aim our redirective efforts at every nook and cranny. One day the struggle will end when our faith will become sight, when we will see in all its splendor Christ's kingdom, "a kingdom of all ages, of all spheres, of all creatures."[7]

Chapter 3

Declaring the Gospel as Public Truth

The United States is now in the midst of a turbulent period in which its people, its elected representatives, and its courts are struggling to define what is meant by the First Amendment right to free exercise of religion. For many interpreters of the First Amendment, religion is seen as something inherently private, restricted to the inner recesses of one's personal life and, perhaps, on Sundays, relegated to the four walls of a church building. Under this interpretation freedom of religion is best described as "freedom of worship." We are free to believe what we will personally and to celebrate it corporately but certainly not to apply it broadly.[1]

This restrictive interpretation, however, misunderstands the nature of religion. Religion is, of course, a matter of the heart, and it necessarily expresses itself in religious gatherings. But true religion also radiates outward into all that a person does. If religion shapes a person's core beliefs and values and cultivates their dispositions and patterns of action, then how could it not affect their political views and public interactions?

For this reason freedom of religion cannot be restricted to freedom of inner worship. It must *necessarily* extend beyond private beliefs and local church worship services. Religion concerns what is publicly true and therefore cannot help but become a matter of public life. This is true of any religion but applies specifically to Christianity. Christianity orients a person's heart toward Christ, a heart orientation that affects the entirety of life, especially a person's actions and interactions in the public square.

Contemporary Western culture, by and large, opts for the restrictive interpretation of religion instead of the more holistic one. As Lesslie Newbigin repeatedly pointed out, secular modernity—his summary term for the assumptions undergirding Western life—*acts* as a religion, and thus many aspects of modernity cannot be reconciled with Christianity.[2] Both Christianity and modernity are inherently missionary faiths, and both make universal claims they understand to be valid for all people everywhere. For years Christian thought leaders have tried to help Christianity survive in the modern world by confining it to the realm of inner experience, by domesticating it so that it doesn't make any claim on public life. Thus what began as a series of tactical retreats has, from our contemporary perspective, turned into a near rout. By privatizing and domesticating Christianity, we marred its central claims—that Christ is the cosmic King and that the gospel is public truth. Newbigin writes:

> When the Church affirms the gospel as public truth it is challenging the whole of society to wake out of the nightmare of subjectivism and relativism, to escape from the captivity of the self turned in upon itself, and to accept the calling which is addressed to every human being to seek, acknowledge, and proclaim the truth. For we are that part of God's creation which he has equipped with the power to know the truth and to speak the praise of the whole creation in response to the truthfulness of the Creator.[3]

The modern mind-set, rooted in the Enlightenment and still regnant among the majority of Western thinkers, finds language like this repugnant and dangerous. Modernity, to be sure, retains a place for public truth *and* a place for religion but not the same place. Truth (with a capital "T"), in the modern mind-set, is only that which can be verified by value-free facts, usually scientific ones. Religion, on the other hand, is understood as the realm of fact-free values. Perhaps no other feature of modernity persists as doggedly as the notion that facts and values do not belong together. Thus, when Christianity is tolerated by contemporary society, usually it is tolerated merely as a realm of values and opinions: it is perfectly fine to believe in Jesus *for yourself* but not to be so haughty as to say that what you believe *is actually and universally true.*[4]

One Cosmic King, One Public Truth in All Spheres of Life

Newbigin was not the only recent theologian arguing, contra modernity, that the gospel is public truth. Abraham Kuyper hammered this point home throughout his career as well. Like Newbigin, Kuyper understood modernism as being at war with Christianity. He recognized that modernity, quite problematically, claimed to provide the master narrative of the world. Long before postmodern critics of modernity would question modernity's presumptuous metanarrative, Kuyper was taking aim at it.

For Kuyper, however, the proper response to modernism was not the way of postmodernism, eschewing master narratives altogether. Rather, Christians were to show that Christianity is "a life-system [worldview] of equally comprehensive and far-reaching power."[5] Instead of viewing metanarratives with suspicion, Christians were to provide a *better* metanarrative. Christianity, Kuyper argued, surpasses the modern worldview in scope, coherency, and intellectual vigor.[6] It accounts not only for private faith and churchly worship but also for public matters such as art, science, commerce, education—and yes, even politics. In other words, the gospel is not merely public truth; it is deeply and abidingly *relevant* truth for every sphere of culture.

At this point, unless you happen to be conversant with Kuyper or Newbigin, this entire perspective might begin to worry you. If the gospel is true—publicly and universally true—outside of the church, doesn't this threaten to demolish our cherished distinction of church and state? Would it not then be most consistent to pursue a theocracy or a church-controlled kingdom of some sort, in which the political realm was brought *directly* under the political headship of the institutional church? In short, how can we claim that the gospel is universally true without making every sphere of life subservient to the church?

"After Their Own Kinds"—Sphere Sovereignty as a Solution to the Theocracy Problem

Kuyper avoided the strict logic of theocracy by appealing to something he called "sphere sovereignty" (for our Dutch-speaking audience, *souvereiniteit in eigen kring,* literally "sovereignty in each circle"). This was Kuyper's way of describing the various dimensions—spheres—of public life and their relationship to one another. As the name implies, Kuyper understood each dimension of life to have an inherent sovereignty, an inner integrity that provided cohesion for that dimension. Jesus Christ was Lord over *every* sphere, but he also ordered each sphere according to distinct patterns.

A key biblical phrase may help illustrate Kuyper's notion: "after their own kinds." In the Genesis account of creation, God makes plants and trees, birds and fish, bugs and livestock and beasts—all *after their own kinds.* Each species follows the pattern God set for it, an ordered pattern that at once displays diversity and unity.

Now imagine that instead of talking about just animals and plants, we extend that principle to dimensions of human life. Scripture, of course, never refers to art, science, and politics as spheres created "after their own kinds" (like the plants and animals), but why should God's dual principles of order and diversity not hold true in these cultural matters just as in the more mundane zoological ones? As Richard Mouw explains, Kuyper's rationale goes "beyond the explicit statements of Scripture to explore larger patterns of coherence that can shed light on the patterns of biblically based thought. . . . There is a fit of sorts between the actual biblical passages they allude to and the more speculative claims."[7]

Order and diversity—this was Kuyper's imaginative and ingenious combination, recognizing that God has ordered every aspect of our lives but has done so in distinct ways. The created orders of art and science, economics and politics, still operate according to their own kinds. Art displays aesthetic excellence while science advances knowledge. Economics exists to steward resources while politics exists to achieve justice. As Gordon Spykman writes, "Each sphere has its own identity, its own unique task, its own God-given prerogatives. On each God has conferred its own peculiar right of existence and reason for existence."[8] And still the one Lord is Lord of them all.

Kuyper's notion of sphere sovereignty also shows us why the institutional church should not seek to control the state. God is sovereign over each of the spheres, *but no sphere is sovereign over the others*. Thus the church should not act as sovereign over art, science, or politics. Neither should the government view itself as sovereign over art, science, or religion. Each sphere has its own integrity and should refrain from encroaching upon the territory of the others. The result is a system of checks and balances—not at the political level by dispersing governmental power but at a deeper, ontological level.[9] So God rules over each sphere but does not do so through the mediation of the institutional church. He does so by means of his ordering word and by means of faithful Christians who use their expertise and energies to help conform those spheres to their God-given design.

That nature of the gospel as public truth means a Christian's engagement with the world must be *total*. Jesus is the Creator of every sphere and the Lord of every sphere. And because he is Lord, we seek to bring every interaction under submission to his lordship. As Newbigin writes:

> The call to the Church is to enter vigorously into the struggle for truth in the public domain. We cannot look for the security which would be ours in a restored Christendom. Nor can we continue to accept the security which is offered in an agnostic pluralism where we are free to have our own opinions provided we agree that they are only personal opinions. We are called, I think, to bring our faith into the public arena, to publish it, to put it at risk in the encounter with other faiths and ideologies in open debate and argument, and in the risky business of discovering what Christian obedience means in radically new circumstances and in radically human cultures.[10]

The gospel is not a private truth to be cordoned off and relegated to our private lives. It is a bold declaration of Christ's lordship over every sphere of life. As Christians, we must see each sphere for what it is—a unique dimension of life ordered according to God's design, yet warped by sin. We must do the hard work of discerning that original design, identifying how it has been corrupted and misdirected by sin, and redirecting each sphere toward Christ. This will not be easy. The cosmic battle is real and will claim more casualties in days to come. But with Christ as our captain, we can and will pursue the risky business of Christian obedience.

Chapter 4

Relating Church and State

Our last chapter introduced the claim of Jesus Christ's universal lordship, a lordship that extends to every sphere of life. The discussion of Christian engagement with the various spheres is a rich area of discussion,[1] but we must bypass most of that discussion to focus in on the two relevant spheres, religion and politics, and two institutions—church and state—related to those spheres.

Secular modernity, for all of its proclamations of tolerance, cannot coexist easily with Christianity because both modernity and Christianity make totalizing claims. They possess competing visions for public life, and while some areas overlap, others come into sharp conflict. A Christianity that is comfortable in the modern context is a Christianity that has had its teeth removed. It is a sham.

The conflict between secular modernity and Christianity is not limited to any one sphere. It extends to the arts, sciences, education, economics, business, and other sectors. But it surfaces in an especially significant manner in the political sphere. Modern governments are the de facto protectors of modern society's political narrative, a narrative based on vague ideas such as "progress" and "equality"—a narrative with strong roots, in fact, in the Christian story. But the moorings have long been jettisoned, and the current political narrative in many ways stands in stark opposition to the Christian vision.

At the core of this conflict is the Christian account of the resurrection. N. T. Wright notes:

> Let me put it starkly. The Bible tells the story of the world as having reached its destiny, its climax, when Jesus of Nazareth came out of the tomb on Easter morning. The Enlightenment philosophy, however, tells the story of the world as having reached its destiny, its climax, with the rise of scientific and democratic modernism. These stories cannot both be true. . . . The point is that the resurrection, if it had occurred, would undermine not only the Enlightenment's vision of a split world but also the Enlightenment's self-congratulatory dream of world history reaching its destiny in our own day and our own systems.[2]

The gospel story is deeply at odds with modern political narratives because each looks to a different place for history's true meaning. Christians look to the event of the resurrection while modern thinkers look to scientific and democratic strategies and methods.

The modern vision can only incorporate Jesus into its view by removing the scandal of the cross and resurrection. The gospel of the cross and resurrection is still "foolishness to the Greeks," to our modern sophisticated culture keepers. Thus modern political narratives push people to sideline religious commitments when debating public matters. If they cannot exterminate Christianity, at least they can shut it up in its own private ghetto.

As we have already argued, this perspective *allows* for Christian faith but only a privatized faith. In response we argue that, although Christianity is deeply personal, it is never merely private. The religious passion may begin in the heart, but it necessarily radiates outward into all of a person's public life, including his political interactions. The Bible will have nothing to do with modernity's hard and fast split between religion and politics. They may be separate spheres, but they have one Lord. Modernity seeks to divorce politics from its Creator, and the result (as in any divorce) is painful and destructive.[3]

But the crucial question remains: *How* should Christians bring their faith commitments to bear in politics? To answer this we look first to the answers given by Jesus, Paul, and Peter. The biblical foundation they provide will show us the appropriate relationship between the church and the state.

Jesus and the State

In an essay on Christianity and the state, N. T. Wright notes what we may easily overlook—that Jesus' life and ministry were pursued in the context of the Roman Empire.[4] For Israel, Rome was the latest in a long line of superpowers, stretching all the way back to Egypt, Babylon, Persia, and Greece. The Jews were offended by Roman rule not only because of its idolatry and burdensome taxation (there is nothing new under the sun) but because Rome was a constant reminder to them of their own sin, which caused them to be exiled in the first place. The deep frustration the Jews felt led them to look longingly for their promised Messiah, the one God had promised would fully restore them from exile. Their God was, after all, the Creator and supreme Ruler of the universe. He would act dramatically on their behalf. And he would do it *politically.*

So when Jesus declared that God's kingdom was at hand (Matt 3:2), everyone heard the obvious meaning: a political kingdom was on the rise. Not one of his audiences envisioned an apolitical series of revival meetings. N. T. Wright writes:

> Jesus' message was after all inescapably political. He
> denounced rulers, real and self-appointed. He spoke of

good news for the poor. He led large groups of people off into the wilderness, a sure sign of revolutionary intent. He announced the imminent destruction of the Jerusalem temple. At the start of a festival celebrating Israel's liberation, he organized around himself what could only have looked like a royal procession. And he deliberately and dramatically acted out a parable of the temple's destruction, thus drawing on to himself the anger of the authorities in a way which he could never have done by healing lepers and forgiving prostitutes (though we should not miss the revolutionary note in his offer of forgiveness, whose real offence lay in its bypassing of the temple cult). . . . He died the death of the *lestai*, the political insurrectionists (Barabbas, and the two crucified with Jesus, were *lestai*). How could he not have been "political"?[5]

Contemporary readers can be forgiven for not seeing the patently political aspect of Jesus' kingdom since he intentionally avoided military might and traditional avenues of power. But from the moment he began his ministry until he was taken up to heaven, Jesus was launching the kingdom God had long ago promised, a kingdom that is deeply and inescapably political.

What, then, are we to think of Jesus' statement to Pilate that his kingdom was "not of this world" (John 18:36)? Certainly not that it was purely ephemeral or a kingdom "of the inner self." Rather, Jesus meant that his kingdom was not like the earthly kingdoms in their sinfulness. His kingdom operates differently, as a kingdom of true justice and real peace. During Jesus' earthly ministry, his kingdom was breaking into the world's political order as a divine rule that comes from outside the earthly realm. So his kingdom is otherworldly, not by being incorporeal but by being divine and righteous. And it is this-worldly in that it breaks into this world's order.[6]

Another oft-misinterpreted statement of Jesus regards the famous dictum of rendering to Caesar what is Caesar's and to God what is God's (Mark 12:13–17). This does not mean, as is often cursorily assumed, that the government rules our physical lives while God rules the spiritual one. It is actually a striking political statement *limiting* Caesar's role and his reign. "Look at this coin," Jesus says. "It's got Caesar's face on it. Fine, he can have it. Give him your money. But *never* give him your ultimate allegiance. That belongs to God alone."

Paul and the State

Like Jesus, Paul's life was lived in the context of the Roman Empire. During his early years he was a Jewish intellectual and activist. But after his dramatic experience on the road to Damascus, he realized that Jesus was the kingdom bringer and lived the rest of his life in light of that fact. How, then, were Christians to live in the midst of another kingdom— Rome—knowing that Jesus had inaugurated a competing kingdom but had not established it in its entirety? How were they to live out ultimate allegiance to Jesus with Caesar still declaring himself lord of the earth? In other words, how should Christians live politically during our present era between Christ's first and second comings?

Significantly, Paul urged the church to realize that Christ was the supreme Lord of the entire universe and that he would return one day to consummate his rule. To the Christians in Philippi (a Roman colony), he wrote that *every* Philippian citizen would one day bow the knee to Jesus and confess that Jesus—not Caesar—is Lord (Phil 2:10–11). To those in Colossae, he wrote that Jesus was the one who created the universe and held it together and who would one day return to renew and restore the fallen universe over which he is Lord (Col 1:15–20). Paul's view of Jesus was no more apolitical than Jesus's view of himself. Christianity was not a strictly religious sect but a rival political vision. As N. T. Wright writes: "Paul's idea of 'proclaiming Christ' had little to do with offering people a new religious option, a new private experience of the love of God, and far more to do with the announcement to the world at large that the crucified and risen Jesus was its Lord and King, the one before whom every knee must bow."[7]

When we proclaim that Jesus rose from the dead and will one day return to consummate his kingdom, *that* is a political message.

But like Jesus, Paul counseled Christians to avoid consummating Jesus' kingdom in the here and now. For example, in his instructions to the Romans, he writes, "Let every person be subject to the governing authorities" (Rom 13:1). Again, this is allegiance, but not *ultimate* allegiance. The Roman church to whom Paul wrote believed Jesus would return—and soon—to take his throne and establish his rightful rule over the world he created.

Paul's instruction in Romans 13 does not remove our future political hope, but it warns the church against anarchy. He warns against an attitude in which Christians could flout the government as if they were above the law. Instead of flouting the government, they should respect the government as a means by which God rules his world. They should realize that, in this fallen world, God mediates his rule through earthly governments who can punish the evil and protect the innocent. Romans 13 does not justify ultimate allegiance to an earthly government, but it does demand Christian respect for an institution that is a part of God's order.

This passage has an interesting application for those of us who live in democratic societies.[8] Political philosopher Richard Mouw writes:

> In modern democracies the power of national leaders is derived from the populace, which is the primary locus of God-given authority. Built into the very process is the possibility of review, debate, reexamination, election, and defeat. Given such a framework, for Christians simply to

acquiesce in a present policy is to *fail to respect* the governing authorities.[9]

For Christians living in the United States, therefore, Paul's instruction to be subject to the governing authorities means we should work for change when our government does not reflect God's best intentions for our society. But more on this later.

Peter and the State

Peter's teaching complements and supplements Paul's. In 1 Peter 2:9–17, he reminds the New Testament church that they are a chosen people, just as Old Testament Israel was a chosen people. Just as Israel was called to be a light to the nations, so is the church.[10] And the way to be a light to the nations, as Peter reveals in this passage, includes pledging allegiance to our earthly governments, living good lives in private and in public, and doing this based on our ultimate allegiance to Jesus Christ. Mouw writes:

> The upshot of Peter's message seems to be this: the people of God are called to have a unique identity among the nations of the earth. They constitute a community whose primary loyalty is to God as revealed in Jesus Christ. But they must seek to work out this loyalty as much as possible within the framework of peaceful relations with civil society.[11]

Peter was warning the church not to take a posture of indifference or insolence toward the government but instead to live Christianly in public. To be publicly righteous glorifies God and benefits the community.

The Church and the State Today

Living as we do in the aftermath of Jesus' first coming and in the hope of his second coming, we must live faithfully in our era and context, just as Paul and Peter did in theirs. We must act out our part of the drama of history, from within our given context, and do so with Christian wisdom and discernment.

While our context differs, the basic principles outlined by Jesus, Paul, and Peter still guide us today. We confess that Jesus is the universal Lord of the whole world (Phil 2:5–11). He inaugurated his kingdom (Matt 3:2) and will one day return to consummate it (Col 1:15–20). His is a kingdom not of this world, meaning it is not warped or distorted by sin (John 18:36), but it manifests in this world because it remains a political—that is, public—kingdom. As we await his return, we are to live out our Christian confession publicly for the common good (1 Pet 2:9–17), respecting government as the divinely intended institution that it is (Rom 13:1), while reserving ultimate allegiance for God alone (Mark 12:1–17).

The American Church and Our Democratic State

How should these principles be applied in a modern democratic republic such as the United States? That is the real trick. Scripture doesn't apply its principles to an American political polity or cultural context. In fact, Scripture doesn't explicitly endorse any one form of government. But Scripture does provide deep-level principles we can apply to our current historical and political context.

Kuyper's notion of sphere sovereignty is helpful again here. Sphere sovereignty, you'll recall, is premised on the belief that God created and ordered every dimension of life. Thus, even if the state posited popular sovereignty (French Revolution) or state sovereignty (German idealists) in the political realm, it was really God who was sovereign in that realm. God ordains every government as a limited remedy for sin's effects, a sort of umpire that maintains order, makes judgments when there are conflicts between spheres, and protects the people.[12]

However, while God is the ultimate sovereign in the political sphere, he still rules that sphere *according to its kind*. Each sphere of human life has its own unique and God-given principles of operation. So the principles that guide government, for instance, are not the same as those operative in the church (or the arts, or economics, etc.). And—this is immensely critical—each sphere has its own *circumference*, a boundary that should not be transgressed by the other spheres.

The relevance of this boundary for the relationship of church and state can hardly be overstated. On one hand, the church should not seek to control the government. But on the other hand, the government should not seek to control the church. That might seem easy enough unless you are familiar with history and recognize how frequent and volatile these border trespasses have been. What makes this balance so difficult to navigate? Perhaps it is the fact that the state does rightly possess a limited jurisdiction over the other spheres, sometimes stepping in as a referee, for example, when one sphere transgresses its boundaries, or in order to protect the weak from the strong within a given sphere. Similarly, the church should rightly possess an organic influence over the other spheres, albeit indirectly, as it disciples its members and then sends them out to bring their cultural activities under Christ's lordship.

Both church and state, therefore, manifest a certain largeness and influence. They are able to impact life in the other spheres. But this largeness and ability to influence also open each sphere up to enormous dangers, the twin errors of statism and theocracy. We must avoid both.

Avoiding Statist Ambitions

Statism occurs when the state oversteps its boundaries by inappropriately interfering with the healthy development of the other spheres. In order to avoid statism in the United States, for instance, we must remind our elected officials that its oversight over the people should have limits. Our society may be plagued by a myriad of problems, but political interference is not the answer to every problem. In other words: *respect your circumference.*

Lest our libertarian readers exult too much, let us clarify: government *should* periodically intrude. By nature of its creational design, government has some responsibilities that should cause it, from time to time, to interfere with the other spheres in a limited manner. Drawing upon Kuyper, Mouw enumerates three such instances:[13]

First, the government may adjudicate inter-sphere disputes, or problems *between* two or more spheres. For example, it may step in between the spheres of business and education by restricting strip clubs from operating on the same block as an elementary school.

Second, the government may adjudicate intra-sphere conflict, or problems *within* a sphere. One common way this is done is by protecting the weak from the strong within any given sphere. It is a sad necessity, for instance, that the government must periodically intrude on the sphere of family, preventing men from abusing their children or wives. Or they might interfere with the sphere of business by keeping an industrial complex from allowing hazardous work conditions.

Third, the government may use its power for certain trans-spherical matters, problems that cannot be adequately addressed within any one sphere. Thus government is justified in taxing us to provide highways and parks and libraries, or in creating occupational health and safety regulations that enrich several other spheres.

But beyond these circumstances the government should be careful not to intrude. It has no business, for instance, regulating the membership of Christian churches or deciding who should or should not be designated as a pastor. It should not attempt to determine which church is a true church and which church is not. Such things are beyond the government's jurisdiction and competence. As Kuyper put it, the government, "must occupy its own place, on its own root, among all the other trees of the forest, and thus it has to honor and maintain every form of life which grows independently in its own sacred autonomy."[14] The state is always at risk of becoming an octopus whose tentacles reach into every aspect of its citizens' lives and which wrap themselves around the other spheres.[15]

Avoiding Theocratic Ambitions

If Christians fear statist trends, our non-Christian friends and neighbors are most fearful of the other extreme—theocracy. But we should share their antipathy. The church, we maintain, oversteps it boundaries by interfering with the healthy development of the other spheres.

One form of theocracy is ecclesiasticism. During the Middle Ages, in many countries, the institutional church had the power to dictate to the state what it should do in matters of public policy. One problem with this situation is that the church is generally incompetent to determine public policy. But the larger problem with theocracy, as Kuyper noted, is that it leads to tyranny.[16] Ironically enough, this tyranny often looks eerily like statism. The state church might begin, for example, to force the government to make laws that effectively require unbelievers to live as if they were believers. Church membership and Christian belief become required at the point of the sword, and the result is a slew of false professions.

The nature of the gospel, we must recall, is that it is *freely* offered and *freely* received. Thus, when some American theologians such as Rousas Rushdoony and Greg Bahnsen promote a form of theocracy known as *theonomy* and argue that Old Testament law should be installed as civil law, we recognize and decry this view as a dangerously inappropriate application of the Bible to our current realities. They want to reinstate the penal sanctions of the Mosaic law in contemporary law—putting blasphemers, adulterers, and liars to death.[17] We reject their theology as a misinterpretation of Jesus' political kingdom.

In response to theocratic ambitions of every stripe, we reaffirm that the political sphere should be free to develop organically under God's sovereignty, rather than being controlled by the institutional church. Christ is the Lord over the spheres, but the institutional church is not. The Bible should shape our political program and public policies today, but God's laws for ancient Israel should not be installed as the law of the land in contemporary America. For this reason, Christians who wish to influence public life in the United States should not do so by trying to install the Bible *en toto* as civil law, forcing unbelievers to act as believers or calling upon the government to let the institutional church dictate policy.

Conclusion

We as Christians must never allow the specter of theocracy to prevent us from shaping public life in light of God's Word. One helpful way to conceive of our task is by recognizing a distinction between the church as an institution and the church as an organism. As a structured institution, the church's mission is to gather for worship, to preach the Word, to share in the Lord's Supper, and other similar activities. The *institutional* church's mission is to make us disciples of Christ rather than to control the state or dictate public policy.

However, the church is not merely an institution. It is also an organism. After the church gathers on the weekend for worship, it scatters organically into all of society. Members of a church find themselves acting and interacting in the public square throughout the week. They find themselves speaking about matters of public life and working for the common good of their fellow citizens. Certain members of the church have the competence and opportunity to shape public policy and should do so by drawing on the wealth of the Christian tradition. And when they seek to influence public life, they should do so by *reasoning* and *persuading* but not by *coercing*.[18]

The Christian's capacity to influence without coercing will become increasingly important as the United States becomes a "post-Christian" nation. We are entering a new era and must prepare ourselves to live as faithful exiles in our own country. To this we now turn.

Chapter 5

Doing Politics in a Post-Christian Country

Over the course of American history, we've had the unique privilege of existing as a nation shaped by a distinctly Christian past. As President Lincoln famously said, ours is a nation "conceived in liberty, and dedicated to the proposition that all men are created equal." Equality for all: this was not some esoteric proposition but the fruit of the Christian tradition.

In fact, many Americans have thought of their nation as a *Christian* nation, founded on Christian moorings and undergirded by Christian principles. This is a contested claim today. More than a few American citizens balk at the notion that the United States is—or ever was—a Christian nation. Thus they emphasize other aspects of our nation's past, bypassing the embarrassing wealth of patently religious language in so much of the public discourse from days gone by. But the reality is unavoidable: Christianity has done great good for our nation.

On the flip side, however, many Christians put too much stock in our nation's Christian identity and history, looking back to earlier days with a naïve sense of nostalgia. They too quickly forget, for example, the horrors of the American slave industry in years past. They also fail to remember that, even though Christianity influenced many of our nation's founders and provided the moral undergirding for our nation's social, cultural, and political development, it was not the only influence. The Enlightenment also wielded great influence, and some of its influential persons and ideas opposed Christianity.

Perhaps it is best to say that the United States has been a predominantly Christian country and that it is now rapidly becoming post-Christian. An increasing number of Americans consider traditional Christian tenets (for example, the doctrine of sin) to be antiquated at best and offensive at worst. Many—perhaps even most—consider basic Christian ethics (for example, Christian teaching about sexual morality) to be restrictive and even harmful and consider evangelical Christians morally inferior at best and reprehensible at worst.

This move away from Christianity has coincided with a demographic change as well. The non-Christian portion of the American citizenry is becoming both numerically larger and increasingly diverse. Religiously, more Americans are identifying as Muslim, Buddhist, Hindu, atheist, or something else. Culturally, too, our diversity continues apace, as immigrants from all over the world continue to answer Lady Liberty's call: "Give me your tired, your poor, your huddled masses yearning to breathe free."

The situation becomes even more complex for Christians when we realize that we live in a democratic republic: the beliefs of the majority directly affect the lives of the minority. And whereas evangelical Christians were once a majority, we now are increasingly a minority.

The good news for Christians is that our faith has never required that we hold positions of power. Christianity, more than any other faith, is uniquely fitted to navigate the complex challenges of being a minority view in a plural society. In fact, Christianity has never been more itself, more consistent with its roots in Jesus himself, than when it stands as a prophetic minority in a culture of pluralism.[1]

In Praise of Pluralism

More than a few people would find our last statement problematic. Political philosopher Donald Zoll, for instance, argues that any group of people awaiting an eschatological utopia will not be able to tolerate the messiness of the here and now.[2] Thus Christianity, as an eschatologically oriented belief system, is incompatible with public plurality, even with democracy itself.

Zoll may be right that certain eschatological visions make civic responsibility in the present nearly unbearable. But not all eschatologies are created equal, and far from ruining our present engagement, the Christian faith uniquely equips us to tolerate—even to *thrive* in—the messy plurality of the here and now. The secret is in the Christian stance toward pluralism.

Pluralism has become something of a dirty word in most Christian circles. But it need not be, provided we are clear on our terms. As philosophers Richard Mouw and Sander Griffioen show us in *Pluralisms and Horizons,* "pluralism" can have six different shades of meaning.[3] They begin by articulating three types of pluralism: (1) *directional pluralism,* referring to the myriad of religions and worldviews that give direction to people's lives; (2) *associational pluralism,* referring to the many possible groups that abound in public life, including families, clubs, and corporations; and (3) *contextual pluralism,* referring to the plurality of our cultural contexts, whether ethnic, gender, class, or economic.

But Mouw and Griffioen do not stop there. Within each type of pluralism, we may further distinguish between *descriptive* and *normative* versions of those three types.[4] The former merely acknowledges the fact of diversity while the latter advocates for it. When we combine these two options with the three aforementioned types of pluralism, we end up with six possible meanings for pluralism:

1. *Descriptive directional pluralism:* highlighting the fact that we have competing views of the direction society ought to go.
2. *Normative directional pluralism:* advocating directional plurality as a good state of affairs.
3. *Descriptive associational pluralism:* highlighting the fact that there are many types of associational patterns.
4. *Normative associational pluralism:* advocating associational plurality as a good state of affairs.
5. *Descriptive contextual pluralism:* highlighting the fact that we exist in a variety of cultural contexts.
6. *Normative contextual pluralism:* advocating contextual plurality as a good state of affairs.[5]

It should be clear that most of these uses are suitable for the Christian. The three descriptive types, for instance, merely define our society as we now know it. Are there a multitude of religions, associations, and cultural contexts? Of course.

We can go further. Because Christians believe God created (and enjoys) the diversity of our cultures, we should have no objection to normative *contextual* pluralism. The gospel, after all, is not a truth contained by one culture alone. Just as a diamond is seen to be more and more radiant with light coming from several directions, so God is seen as more and more radiant with the praise of various cultures, tongues, peoples, and nations (Rev 5:9).

Nor should we find normative *associational* pluralism intolerable. People gather around similar interests. We distinguish between *families* and *neighbors* and *coworkers.* A great deal of the joy of the natural human life is found in the diversity of associations we experience.

But a bogey remains in the mix. Normative *directional* pluralism can find no cozy companionship with the Christian faith. We acknowledge the various worldviews present in our society, but we also acknowledge that these worldviews lead in patently different directions.

It is, therefore, impossible to consistently promote this type of pluralism. Worldview structures promote an all-encompassing vision of the world, replete with judgments about truth and error, right and wrong. Absolute relativism (which is what this type of pluralism amounts to) attempts to downplay the obvious difference between worldviews. As Christian believers, we cannot take this type of relativism seriously, as it undermines central tenets of our faith.

Directional Plurality in the Public Square

At this point a reader like Zoll might suspect that we have painted ourselves into a corner. "All well and good," he might say, "Christians *acknowledge* directional pluralism. I'll concede that much. But you don't like it. You don't want it. The inevitable result is that you'll find yourself wanting to do everything in your power—even employing coercion—to redirect society toward *your* view."

However, we respond that the Christian faith actually restrains us from trying to do everything in our power to redirect people to our view. Although, regretfully, too many Christians have coerced others throughout our history, we maintain that such coercion is not inherent to a rejection of directional pluralism. Nor is it consistent with the pattern of our Lord, who rather than forcing others to believe in him, laid down his life as a demonstration of the gospel.

Because of Christ's example, Christianity enables its adherents to tolerate plurality in a way that other worldviews find more difficult. For several years I (Chris) lived in a Muslim country under the sway of Sharia law. Many Muslims I met were dissatisfied with the Islamic view of the good life and would feel comfortable sharing their doubts and questions with me, a foreigner. But *never* would they have voiced any dissident voice in a public arena out of fear that the local imam (Islamic religious teacher) would enact swift punishments.

The Christian approach ought to stand in stark contrast to this inflexible coercion. But a person like Zoll would be right about one thing: we do not *like* or *want* our society pointed in idolatrous directions. So how can Christians apply their deepest religious beliefs in a public square that is crowded with those of other worldviews, religions, and ideologies without browbeating others to conform to our views?

The answer is by no means obvious. In fact, a myriad of possible answers have been offered through the years, some in diametric opposition to one another. We present three such answers amid this panoply, commending the third as, in our estimation, the most faithful.

A Naked Public Square?

One powerfully influential answer to the "Christianity and the public square" question comes from an American political philosopher named John Rawls.[6] Rawls argues that American citizens should make decisions about social and political matters from behind a "veil of ignorance." We should pretend that we do not know our own religious commitments, race, or socioeconomic status, allowing our arguments to stand on their own two feet. Rawls argues for a "thin theory of the good," rejecting any significant role for "thick" elements, such as religion, morality, and philosophy. Or, to use another analogy, we should all approach the public square naked, shorn of precommitments and assumptions.[7]

Central to Rawls's thesis is the assumption that we can—and should—separate our public self from our private self. You may be a Christian at home but must merely be a citizen in public. Rawls's solution, however, is flawed. First, and most fundamentally, Rawls wrongly assumes that one can separate one's private and public self. This is impossible, and those who promote it are blind to the deep wedding of public and private selves in their own hearts. Rawls himself is the perfect example of the inseparability: like every other human soul, he has some intractable ideological commitments he simply would never lay aside—such as his commitment to democratic liberalism. These commitments drive his public interaction. In other words, Rawls has come to the public arena (thank God) fully clothed.

Laying aside the impossibility of Rawls's proposal, however, we Christians must reject it on theological grounds as well. We confess that Jesus Christ is Lord *of all.* The scope of his lordship is not incidental and precludes us from abandoning our religious commitments just because we are acting publicly. Besides, even if our opponents do not share our convictions, we continue to believe that the Christian perspective offers vitality and hope, that the Christian tradition is not merely meaningful for *us* personally but also healthy for *society* as a whole. It provides a vantage point from which to critique the government when it has overstretched its arm, to prevent patriotism from becoming national chauvinism, to stop us from expressing our deepest convictions in mean-spirited ways.[8] Why would we willfully hide what we know would enrich our neighbors? To even attempt approaching the public square without Christian raiment is to love our neighbors less than we should.

A Theocratic Public Square?

At the other end of the spectrum are theocratic ambitions. Theocracy is a notoriously ambiguous concept that gets tossed around as an accusation against all sorts of Christian proposals. In this chapter we are employing the word to mean "a form of state in which the leaders see themselves as ruling on behalf of God in a way that subverts sphere sovereignty." Now, to be fair, not many Christian proposals rise to the level of theocracy, in our opinion.

However, historically, many Western countries have subscribed to a form of theocracy we call *ecclesiasticism*, in which the church exceeds its own authority by controlling the other spheres. Additionally, even today in the United States, some theologians have proposed a form of theocracy called *theonomy*. These theonomists, including some Catholics (like David Schindler) and Protestants (Rousas Rushdoony, Greg Bahnsen) argue that Old Testament law (and its penalties for crime) should be installed as law today in America.[9]

In any case theocracy does not provide a viable alternative to the naked public square. As we saw in the last chapter, theocracy is an opposite error of statism. It ought to be rejected because it confuses the boundaries between religion and politics and between church and state. In other words, theocracy forces religion to reach beyond its God-given boundaries. But theocracy is *also* the opposite error to the naked public square. Whereas the naked public square tries to split our private and public selves squarely in two, theocracy foolishly attempts to fuse them. The result is worse for both the public and the private spheres.

A Convictional and Plural Public Square?

Both of the aforementioned views emphasize a truth but elevate that truth too far. The naked public square treasures plurality while theocracy preaches convictional uniformity. But both are necessary. The public square should be both *convictional* (contra Rawls) and *plural* (contra theocrats). If we were able to combine convictional Christianity with principled pluralism, we could achieve a view that allows Christians to retain their convictions without trampling on others.

Convictional Christianity

The public square should be, first of all, convictional. In his insightful book *The Naked Public Square*, Richard John Neuhaus argues, as we have here, that it is impossible to have a truly naked public square. People simply cannot divest themselves of their most deeply held beliefs.[10] "The public square," Neuhaus writes, "will not and cannot remain naked. If it is not clothed with the 'meanings' born by religion, new 'meanings' will be imposed by virtue of the ambitions of the modern state."[11] The real question is not whether to bring our religious beliefs into politics, but how to do so in a helpful rather than harmful manner.

The alternative is to abandon the public square to an alternate belief system. As Neuhaus writes, "When religious transcendence is excluded, when the public square has been swept clean of divisive sectarianisms, the space is opened to seven demons aspiring to transcendent authority. As with a person so also with a society, the last condition is worse than the first."[12] Rawls's secular liberalism, for example, is a jealous god. It establishes itself as a dogma and allows no room for other dogmas.

We cannot simply sideline our most deeply ingressed beliefs. We cannot remove our heart, in the religious sense of the word, any more than we can remove it in the physical sense. After all, as Neuhaus often said, "Public life is mainly about culture, and at the heart of culture is morality, and at the heart of morality is religion."[13] Instead of trying to do so, Neuhaus argues, we should allow our Christian beliefs to inform our views on social, cultural, and political issues. Our Christian beliefs should always inform our views, even though we may not always articulate our views publicly in an explicitly Christian manner.

Principled Pluralism

With convictional Christianity we should also promote a principled pluralism for the American public square. Referring back to the categories provided by Mouw and Griffioen, we affirm associational and contextual plurality as necessary corollaries of God's created order. God built into the world a splendid diversity that finds its unity in him. He created humanity as social and cultural beings who would bring out the diverse potentials hidden in his good creation. No wonder there is such a profusion of cultural contexts and associations: God intended it.

We also must recognize that, prior to Christ's return, there will continue to be directional plurality. So we must make a certain *provisional* peace with it. Although it is an alien intruder, a party crasher in God's good creation, it is here to stay until the Lord returns. We cannot pull up the weeds without destroying the wheat as well. And not only will there always be two types of people—those who worship Christ and those whose affections are fixed on false gods and idols—but there will be a profusion of variations even within those two categories.

Instead of trying to neutralize or flatten this plurality, we should do our best to put it to work for the common good. As Christians, we challenge our fellow citizens to put their convictions and their particularity to work for the common good, and we ourselves put our convictions to work in a way that safeguards the public interest rather than merely our own tribal interest. Similarly, we challenge our legislative, executive, and judicial branches to foster a political environment that does not actively promote secular zealotry (or any other type of zealotry), just as it does not promote Christian theocracy. The government should not actively promote beliefs of any kind—religious or irreligious—that deny religious liberty and promote the interests of the few over the interests of the many.

As Christians, we must be both faithful and flexible, as Richard Mouw once put it.[14] As *faithful* Christian citizens, we must never recant our beliefs or act unethically because of pressure put upon us by fellow citizens. But as *flexible* Christian citizens, we must accept the limitations of living in a country composed of fellow citizens who do not share our vision of the good life. We should accept the right opportunities for political cooperation with other citizens and should not be surprised when no such opportunity is available. But these two only work when paired together: flexibility without faithfulness is relativism, but faithfulness without flexibility is utopian idealism.

Desiring the Heavenly City

Above all, we must pray for Christ's kingdom to come. Indeed, all of our public actions are, or should be, enacted prayers for the consummation of God's kingdom. Our public activism should be the physical manifestation of our spiritual prayer to God, a tangible expression of, "God, make it so *here* as it is in heaven!" This is the basis of our conviction, what Mouw and Griffioen call "a particularized yearning for a new kind of public arena," one that will be seen in its fullness only on the last day. Every engagement with politics in the present age must be "seen against the background of the eternal horizon of the Heavenly City."[15] We hope, we pray, and we act in such a manner that our nation might be able to see signs of that Heavenly City in our day—here, now. But our ultimate hope is always there, always then—until these dim reflections fade and we see face-to-face.

Chapter 6

Cultivating Wisdom and Public Virtue

As we have seen thus far, we evangelical Christian citizens of the United States find ourselves in an increasingly minority role. Our vision of the good life now competes with many other visions. And in the midst of this plurality, we should allow the biblical narrative to shape our response to politics. By operating within the Christian framework of principled pluralism, we can foster an environment conducive to human flourishing—avoiding statism, theocracy, naked public squares, and a host of other ills.

But even once we have established this Christian framework for principled pluralism, many practical questions remain to be answered and issues remain to be addressed. The political realm is so complex and nuanced (by nature) and messy (because of sin) that we need to cultivate wisdom and pray for virtue in order to navigate it faithfully. We need wisdom because most public policy decisions are not addressed explicitly in Scripture. And we need virtue since we speak as followers of Christ and claim to bring words of grace and life. It is ironic—and sadly all too common—when we set forth a Christian proposal but do so in an unchristian manner.

So before we turn to some specific questions in public life today, we stop to consider what it might mean for Christians to approach politics with wisdom and virtue. We pause here long enough to note six ways our political engagement can—indeed, must—be governed by Christian wisdom and virtue.

1. Seeking the Good of the City

When the people of Israel were exiled to Babylon, God didn't call them to armed revolution. Instead he called them to work for the good of their new city. In Jeremiah 29:5–7, he says to Israel:

> Build houses and dwell in them; plant gardens and eat their fruit. Take wives and beget sons and daughters; and take wives for your sons and give your daughters to husbands, so that they may bear sons and daughters—that you may be increased there, and not diminished. And *seek the peace of the city* where I have caused you to be carried away captive, and pray to the LORD for it; for in its peace you will have peace. (NKJV, emphasis added)

This passage portrays a uniquely Judeo-Christian approach to citizenship.[1] Avoiding cultural accommodation on the one hand and sectarian withdrawal on the other, the Jews were called to *serve* the city of Babylon while still maintaining an identity *separate from* the city. The peace of Babylon, pagan though it may be, would mean peace for Israel as well.

Christians should see themselves as alien residents. We are residents of this created world and of the cities we live in. God planted us here, and we should serve our cities and countries. However, we are "alien" residents, in that we will not be truly at home in this world until Christ returns to renew and restore it, to purge it of sin and sin's consequences.

Our feet can be firmly planted on American soil, but our eyes will also be firmly fixed on the future kingdom.

This view of ourselves as alien residents, oddly enough, provides us with the only possible way to provide our society with a preview of Christ's future reign of peace and justice. Because our lives are shaped primarily by the biblical narrative instead of the predominant cultural narrative of our day, Christians will always seem a little bit strange to society. The world, of course, is quick to assume that it is our *Christianity* that is off-kilter. But the biblical narrative reminds us that *this fallen world* is off-kilter and will remain so until Christ returns to set it aright.

C. S. Lewis depicts this interestingly in his magnificent space trilogy. His main character, Ransom, meets with creatures called "eldila," something similar to angels. But whenever they appear—as beams of lights—they are slightly tilted, not quite at a right angle to the ground. Yet Ransom, in their presence, senses that it is not the *eldila* who are askew. It is rather the earth itself. They are upright; he is crooked.[2]

It is the same with us. The biblical narrative may look tilted to those who are not Christians, but, if so, they have it backwards. It is, in fact, the only available portrayal of "upright," the standard by which sin's crookedness can be made straight and true. And as we seek to live according to the shape of Scripture, we provide a chance for our society to flourish, to regain some of that *shalom* that was lost when our first parents sinned.

2. Living Realistically in a Time Between the Times

As we work for the good of our country and its public life, we should continually remind ourselves to be realistic in our expectations. We live in a fallen world, one that will not be conformed fully to Christ's ideals until he returns. We should not expect more from politics and public life than can be had in this time between the times. Investing politics with majestic hopes will only lead to crushing disappointment.

As we have argued repeatedly, this does not mean we abandon politics. Rather, we labor dutifully, all the while knowing that our ultimate hope comes not through the right political leader but through Christ alone. Good politics won't save us from what ails us most; neither will bad politics take away what matters most.

We understand the anxiety with which many conservative Christians in America perceive the climate around them. Here is our country, a country we want to share our values, a country that *did* at one time largely share those values. And right here in our backyard, we think, we are now treated as interlopers. But two words are needed in response to this anxiety (an anxiety often leading to anger or fear). First, the situation is not altogether as bad as it often seems. Every generation senses that it is a half step away from utter destruction, but God continues to show patience. The common grace manifest in our society slows any descent into chaos. Second, a power remains at work in our society that can redeem and restore—the gospel. We need not view our country's future with *optimism* in order to live with *hope.* Optimism often is not grounded in any reality. But Christian hope is grounded in reality and enables us to live with grace and joy even in times of distress and darkness.

As Christians we know the story's end, and no disagreement in the present can cast a long shadow over that shining truth. Thus, even as we engage in serious and sustained debate with the majority of our fellow citizens, we do so with an eye toward the new heavens and earth. Our fellow citizens should sense that we care deeply about current politics. But they should also be unsettled, seeing how we consider every jot and tittle of current politics penultimate to the coming of our Lord.

3. Being Shaped for Public Righteousness and Civility

In his book *Uncommon Decency*, Richard Mouw argues that Christian churches should be formation centers for righteousness—not merely private righteousness (manifest, for instance, in our personal devotions) but public righteousness.[3] Specifically, he argues that churches should teach their members a commitment to civility. "Civility," Mouw writes, "is public politeness. It means that we display tact, moderation, refinement and good manners toward people who are different from us."[4] We hold our convictions, but out of love for our neighbor and concern for our witness, we hold them in a gracious and kind manner.

In the charged climate of contemporary politics, civility truly is a lost virtue. Those persons most passionate on any issue, it would seem, feel duty-bound to leave civility at the door. But we find this incivility distasteful and insist that it is possible—more than possible, commendable—for our public lives to be marked by both conviction and civility.

Civility's black eye comes from the faulty assumption that those who are civil in their public disposition must necessarily be "soft." Politeness implies that we like everyone and agree with them. But nothing could be further from the truth. The essence of civility is not spinelessness but self-control; it is the capacity to show love and grace *particularly when* we disagree with others and even when we dislike them. Thus Israel was instructed to be hospitable to sojourners and aliens, even though the recipients of their hospitality did not share their faith commitments. And New Testament believers are encouraged to honor everyone (1 Pet 2:17), living peaceably with all (Rom 12:18). Their civility was not contingent on agreement. It was, rather, practiced against a backdrop of assumed *disagreement.*

Civility has two sides. The first is civil *speech.*[5] One of the ugliest aspects of public life in America is the way many politicians, pundits, and citizens speak about those on the other side of the aisle. We demonize those with whom we disagree. Not content to disagree with them, we speak of them disparagingly, implying that they are not only wrong but evil.

Christians should have no part in such ungodliness. It offends God, tarnishes our witness, and undermines our ability to gain the trust of our fellow citizens. Verbal incivility signals to a watching world that we are like everybody else, that we are ideologues whose primary goal is to gain power for ourselves at any cost. But verbal civility, undergirded by genuine Christian love and concern, signals that while Christians are a strange people, we are also a good people, whose primary goal is to contribute to the common good by being ambassadors for the King.

Similarly, public righteousness necessitates a civil *attitude*. A civil attitude is more than niceness, although it includes niceness. As Mouw argues, it also includes being empathetic toward others, curious about their life experiences and perspectives, and genuinely ready to learn from others.[6] This includes our speech, of course, but extends beyond it to a general way of life. Thus we insist on listening to our opponent's arguments, not merely to counter them but also to truly understand. And even as we argue with passion, we open ourselves to correction. Even though Scripture is not wrong, our particular interpretations and applications of it to the public square may well be wrong. It is a mark of strength, not weakness, to admit an error and to learn from it. Those with uncivil attitudes are, above all else, poor learners.

4. Taking a Longer and Broader View

If the current social and political climate has provoked in evangelical Christians feelings of anxiety and fear, it has also led to impatience. We want to see change, and we want to see change *now,* so we often put too much of our hope in short-term political activism. Thus we lean too heavily on social media activism, for example, or concerted efforts to overwhelm the switchboards of our local congressman. These types of activism are not wrong (both, at times, can be timely and appropriate measures), but the results are necessarily short-lived and superficial. If our political strategy is relegated to this sort of activism, we have already lost.

We need to remind ourselves to take a longer and broader view, to work toward a sustained and comprehensive cultural witness over generations. After all, politics is only one sphere of culture. Even if we were to completely reform that sphere to reflect God's kingdom (a mammoth "if"), we would fail to take into account the myriad other ways society is affected through other spheres. Politics, in other words, is not the headwater of culture. In many ways politics stands downstream from culture, *reflecting* our society at least as often as it *directs* our society.

So if we want to influence our society, our efforts must not be aimed only at short-term fixes, *especially* if we are limiting our scope to politics. We must expend our energies in every sphere of culture, recognizing that human life is an integrated whole. There is no "trickle-down" method when it comes to impacting society; we must aim everywhere at once.

Consider, for instance, the influence that we might have on our country through shaping the minds and hearts of our own children, grandchildren, and extended families. The time we spend investing in them will reap untold dividends in the future. As G. K. Chesterton said, "How can it be broad to be the same thing to everyone, and narrow to be everything to someone?" The task of child-rearing, he insists, "is laborious, but because it is gigantic, not because it is minute."[7]

Or consider the power of the arts (not just "high art" but popular media such as music, television, and movies) to shape the way entire cultures and subcultures think and feel about issues. Are we really content to abandon this field to others, to limit ourselves to defending truth while caring nothing for beauty?

Or consider the influence schools and universities have in shaping the worldviews of young men and women. In our opinion Christian schools and universities often merely pay lip service to the notion of "Christian education," conforming in large part to the ideologies set by other universities. The "Christian" aspect of their schooling is a veneer of some sort, a chapel attendance requirement, a perfunctory prayer to start each class, or a system of 1950s-era dating guidelines. But if Christian scholars and teachers would put forth a sustained effort to shape their research, writings, and teaching *in light of a biblical worldview,* the positive results in the lives of our students would be remarkable.

The broader and longer view means investing long-term in every aspect of American culture—art, science, education, politics, economics, business, sports, and family life. It means avoiding the pitfall of social and political passivity, on the one hand, and mindless and ineffective short-term activism, on the other hand.

5. Choosing Between Thick and Thin

In his book *The Interpretation of Cultures*, anthropologist Clifford Geertz promotes a helpful concept called "thick description." As he describes it, a thick description of human behavior is one that explains not just behavior but the context of the behavior, such as the beliefs, feelings, and values operative in a particular culture. The opposite is a "thin description," one that is divorced from such contextual factors. The concept of thick description has now found its home in the humanities—in fields such as politics, philosophy, and theology. In the context of Christianity, a "thick" description will appeal to religious arguments overtly, while a "thin" one will use more generic language.[8]

Christians will have to make decisions about how "thick" their language is when interacting in the public square. When engaging in discussion about a certain political issue, we must discern whether it is advantageous to use patently Christian terms and when to use more "neutral" ones. Will we make our argument while appealing publicly to Christian revelation or doctrine (e.g., decrying abortion because the child is made in God's image), or will we appeal more to common assumptions and shared ideals (e.g., analyzing the deleterious psychological effects of abortion on the mothers who seek it)? Wisdom will dictate which to use and will vary subject to subject, occasion to occasion, audience to audience.

In distinguishing between thick and thin language, however, we must remember that our arguments should *always* be based in Christian thought, even if they are not always communicated publicly in explicitly Christian terms. What differs is not whether we are applying Christianity but whether we make that application manifest and obvious. In other words, we are always "thick" in our thinking though not always in our expression. Or, to use Neuhaus's illustration, we always approach the public square fully clothed; but we need not, for that reason, wear our loudest suit.

There are few black-and-white rules when weighing which language to use—thick or thin. As Mouw notes, this decision can be a thorny business: "Messiness will . . . attend our efforts to sort through the merits of 'thick' and 'thin' language as we engage in our public discourse. What we say when we are addressing the issues of public life, and how and when we say it, are questions that can be answered only by a continuing reliance on discernment."[9]

Both thick and thin languages have specific benefits *and* specific risks. Thick language may be clearer but can ostracize those who reject religious tradition. Thin language may gain a wider audience but can lose some of the power and precision of speaking within the framework of Christian teaching. What is appropriate discussing one issue may be folly when discussing another—or when discussing the same issue with a different audience. Mouw is right: we must pray for wisdom in deciding between thick and thin.

6. Politicking in the Pulpit (or Not)

Here is a blunt question sure to stir up trouble at your next dinner party: *Should pastors preach politics from the pulpit?* Some Christians, of course, consider the practice wrong in all cases: "The pulpit is for preaching the Word!" Others respond by saying, "But the Word is full of social, cultural, and political matters." Our answer, were we invited to your dinner party, is: "Yes and no." But mostly no.

Yes, Christianity is a deeply political religion. The gospel message declares that Jesus is Lord of all, and his dominion touches on every aspect of public life. Thus we find in Scripture teachings relevant to public disputes today—about sexuality, financial ethics, compassion for the poor, the value of human life, and a hundred other issues. But the Bible refrains from giving comprehensive and specific policy directives for us today. We should be profoundly grateful for this.

Because the Bible allows room for application regarding politics, we must be exceedingly careful in addressing matters of public policy from the pulpit. If we decide to make that connection, we must be confident our words and concerns mirror those of God. As Mouw suggests, if we have such a confidence, we might speak directly to a situation and offer our opinion. But this should be rare. The usual pattern, rather, should be merely to raise the questions and encourage the Christians who have competence in that realm to find an answer.[10]

When exercised judiciously and rarely, a church's public stance on a matter of public policy can be a powerful statement. But the church's greatest influence on public life will come through the power of the preached Word as it shapes its members to live righteous lives.

Conclusion

Engaging in the public square, like all worthwhile endeavors, is no easy venture. In fact, the pattern of wisdom and virtue outlined here will be *impossible* for us under our own power. We cannot, of ourselves, seek the good of our nation, take a longer view, or respond with grace when impugned. Insofar as we attempt to apply Christian principles to public life in our own strength, we will fail.

But we are not driven merely by Christian *principles*. We are driven by the Christian *gospel*. With Paul we confess that "Christ Jesus came into the world to save sinners, of whom I am the foremost" (1 Tim 1:15). The heart behind every political action, for the Christian, is the simple yet endlessly relevant truth, that because he died for us, we will live for him. Wisdom and virtue are not attitudes we cultivate abstractly, in isolation from the biblical story. They are grateful responses to a Savior who took our place on Calvary's cross.

Interlude

The following seven chapters pick up relevant issues in the twenty-first century United States, attempting to show how Christians might approach each issue in a distinctly Christian manner. How should we think about, talk about—even *vote* about—issues like abortion, economic policies, and race relations?

To attempt such an endeavor immediately runs the risk of implying that there is *one* way to answer and approach each issue—or, even worse, that one particular political party conforms to the kingdom of God. But cable network blather notwithstanding, Jesus simply cannot be co-opted into a cause. Jesus remains an equal opportunity offender, issuing challenges to every person and to every political party. Thus what follows, while manifestly political, is far from a political manifesto. Republicans, Democrats, Independents—all of us—have much to learn, even to repent of.

We also wish to point out—yes, again—that Christians (not to mention the rest of our society) can and will disagree on these issues. And even if we agree on broad principles, specific applications can easily become contentious. Thus we must manifest what Richard Mouw aptly calls "uncommon civility."[1] Disagreement may be strong and convictional, but it need not therefore devolve into spite, anger, and hate. Let us show the world the lost art of disagreeing firmly while still loving deeply.

Our differences, however, are not immaterial. What is at stake in each of the following issues has real consequences and demands our disciplined reflection. If we care about the good of our society (which we do), then we must apply wisdom and virtue to the questions of our day. We must display grace rather than venom. We must seek truth and censure error. We must take a long and broad view, enacting comprehensive rather than superficial solutions. We must be discerning about our language, choosing between "thick" and "thin" argumentation.

Above all, we must remain realistic in our political expectations, knowing that our true hope is only in the coming kingdom. Thus we look forward, always forward, but not as the world does. The world latches on to the future with desperation, yearning for a better life but lacking any grounds for true hope. But as we look forward, we soberly and confidently await the new heavens and new earth. And we pray, in the midst of today's most contentious issues, that our efforts, halting and imperfect though they may be, might play some small part in that final revelation.

Chapter 7

Life and Death

Few political issues in the United States are as divisive and impassioned as those relating to life and death. For example over the past several decades, debates about abortion have in large part acted as a litmus test for social conservatism or liberalism. We place this issue at the front of our practical survey because we consider the public policy decisions surrounding these debates to be of enormous significance.

We begin by providing a biblical view of life and death, then follow that overview with a public debate regarding life and death between Christian thought leader Richard John Neuhaus and the secular ethicist Peter Singer. From Neuhaus we will gain insight into how we might make the case of the sanctity of life during our own day.

A Biblical View of Life and Death

On the face of it, the biblical case regarding life and death should be one of the simplest ethical questions to answer: in the Sixth Commandment we are told, "You shall not murder" (Exod 20:13). This command, however, is situated within a larger biblical picture.

God is, we will recall, the Creator, Sustainer, and Lord of all life. He gave the "breath of life" to every creature (Gen 1:30), particularly to humanity (Gen 2:7). And humanity occupies a special relationship to God as his image bearers, our lives reflecting something of our Maker's own life. Yet Adam and Eve's sin precipitated a new reality: death. Because of sin, we all—like Adam—experience death, both spiritual and physical. It is the sheer mercy of God that he sent his Son to taste the full measure of *death* in our place so that we might *live* eternally with him (Rom 6:2–4).

Because God takes pleasure in the life he has given, death grieves him. He expresses deep displeasure when one human being takes the life of an innocent other (Gen 4:10–11). He reminds us that murder offends him specifically because it is an affront to God's own image (Gen 9:5–6). God looks on every member of humanity with a more tender compassion than a mother looks on her own newborn child, and he agonizes over their every pain.

The New Testament condemnation of murder does not substantially differ from the Old except that Jesus deepens and extends the scope of the prohibition (Matt 5:21–26). Thus from cover to cover, the Bible affirms that human life is God's good creation, whereas death is always an unwelcome intruder.

Abortion

Scripture does not explicitly mention abortion, but it does speak clearly enough about human life in the womb for us to know that we are prohibited from taking the life of an unborn baby. The psalmist argues that God creates the unborn and knows them intimately and individually, just as he knows adults (Ps 139:13–16). The biblical writers use personal pronouns to describe unborn children (Matt 1:20–21); note that God consecrates them for special service even while they are in the womb (Luke 1:41; Gal 1:15) and considers their death just as serious as the death of an adult (Exod 21:22–25).[1]

Apart from Scripture, scientific and medical rationales should lead us to view unborn babies as human.[2] According to modern genetics, for instance, when a mother's egg is fertilized by the father's sperm, an individual distinct from either parent comes into existence. And contemporary medical technology, such as 3-D ultrasounds, makes the humanity of the unborn even more vivid.

The historical argument bolsters that of Scripture, science, and medicine. The Old Testament Torah is joined by the Hippocratic Oath and the Code of Hammurabi in explicitly defending the life of the unborn. And while these law codes represent the most sophisticated laws of their time, they represent the majority stream of history: societies throughout history have been overwhelmingly opposed to the practice of elective abortion.

Many proponents of legalized abortion consider the fetus to be "less than" human or only "potentially" human. Ambiguous discussions regarding "personhood" are brought forward in order to question whether an unborn human deserves this worthy moniker. If not, then the budding human life assumes a different category (not yet a person) than those humans already born. Because the baby is not yet self-conscious, "it" is not yet a person. Killing persons is bad; killing nonpersons is acceptable. The argument from consciousness is wrong and can be seen as wrong when we realize that adult humans are not self-conscious when they are in a state of dreamless sleep. And we do not consider sleeping humans to be nonpersons.

Other abortion advocates argue that the baby is a part of the mother and that the mother has every right to have part of her body removed. This makes elective abortion a question of privacy, not of life or death. Such was the argument, for instance, in *Roe v. Wade*. Yet *Roe* notwithstanding, this argument fails to do justice to the baby's *uniqueness*. Even before birth unborn children have their own brain waves, blood types, body shapes, and unique genetic identities. The child may reside *inside* her mother, but to insist that she is no more than an appendage to be removed at will violates both scientific evidence and common sense.

Many elective abortion advocates, however, take a softer stance. They might admit that abortion "prevents a life," but they desire this freedom for exceptional cases—most notably, incest and rape.[3] We acknowledge that many pregnancies take place under difficult circumstances, sometimes even tragic circumstances. And women who have been assaulted deserve our full sympathy, compassion, and protection. But killing a child does nothing to offer compassion to hurting women. No child should be punished in that manner for the sins of his father.

Euthanasia and Physician-Assisted Suicide

So far the question of death *at the end* of life warrants less public discussion in contemporary American debate than the question of death at the beginning of life, but the issue of euthanasia is significant and might soon press to the forefront of public debate. Many argue that it is acceptable, even preferable, for a suffering person to die. This may occur either indirectly or directly—either a doctor *equips* his "patient" to die (physician-assisted suicide) or does the deed himself (euthanasia). The rationale given generally involves ending a person's suffering or a low quality of life.[4]

Scripture gives no indication that such motivations warrant killing. Insofar as suicide and assisted suicide are directly addressed in Scripture, both are prohibited (1 Sam 31:4; Judg 9:54). God created life, and he values it whether we share his valuation or not. While there are instances in which God allows—even commands—people to take the lives of others *justly*, there is no indication that God desires us to end lives because their quality is "too low." Aiming to kill a patient is neither compassionate nor morally permissible.

The extrabiblical evidence against euthanasia corroborates this judgment. Societies who permit such killing, for instance, are feeling the predictable effects of their actions—guilt.[5] And if this logic is allowed to take hold, it is a short step from *voluntary* suicides to *involuntary* ones. After all, if innocent lives *can* be ended, there are times when, in fact, they *must* be.[6] Some argue that this is paranoia. Sadly, however, involuntary euthanasia is already on the rise.[7] And in the Netherlands (where euthanasia is legal), thousands of elderly citizens carry cards prohibiting doctors from euthanizing them, while others fear going in for basic medical care because of the possibility of euthanasia.[8]

A Public Debate: Richard John Neuhaus and Peter Singer

An interesting case study concerning life-and-death issues is a debate at Colgate University (November 2001) between Richard John Neuhaus and Peter Singer. The topic: "Who Should Live, and Who Should Die?"

Neuhaus, the founding editor of *First Things* magazine, had been a well-known theological and political liberal who became a conservative in the aftermath of the *Roe v. Wade* decision (though, in his estimation, he didn't shift; the parties did). Having marched with Martin Luther King Jr. during the civil rights movement, Neuhaus viewed the protection of the unborn as itself a significant civil rights issue. He would later call legalized abortion "the single greatest threat to the moral legitimacy of this political order."[9]

Singer, on the other hand, is a Princeton University ethicist known for his radical revisioning of the traditional ethic of human life and death. A hardened atheist, he dismisses the notion of God-given human dignity. "By 2040," he notes, "it may be that only a rump of hard-core, know-nothing religious fundamentalists will defend the view that every human life, from conception to death, is sacrosanct."[10]

For Singer the moral status of a human being is defined by consciousness and functionality.[11] Those who are *most* conscious and functional have more worth—and moral status—than those who are less conscious and functional. Healthy teenagers, for instance, have a higher status than babies, the elderly, or certain severely disabled persons.

Because of this consciousness/functionality rubric, Singer views certain *nonhuman* animals as having a higher moral status than certain humans. An adult chimpanzee, for instance, might have a higher status than a human child with Down syndrome. Thus, as Singer argues, infanticide is in certain instances commendable while killing certain animals is not.[12]

In the debate at Colgate, Neuhaus argued that human beings are responsible to their broader community and that responsibility dictates they should not kill innocent human beings. By contrast, Singer argued that his ethic centered on reducing suffering and respecting people's preferences. Such an ethic permits killing any number of humans, including unborn infants, certain born infants, and patients in a vegetative state.

It should be clear that we resonate with Neuhaus's perspective rather than Singer's. But several features of the debate itself warrant specific mention.

First, knowing that Singer placed no value in patently scriptural reasoning, Neuhaus attempted to show the societal harms of Singer's position. Singer's ethic, Neuhaus posited, sounded hauntingly familiar to the Nazi doctrine of "life unworthy of life"—the very reason Singer is not welcome at German universities. If an unborn baby is allowed to be killed four weeks before birth, why not four weeks after? What, Neuhaus asked, would logically prevent the systematic killing of all deemed too frail to be useful? In short, Neuhaus consistently drew attention to the fact that Singer's ethic, though consistent and logical, led to an end that nearly every listener would find objectionable. Neuhaus was fighting for the good of his city and taking a long view and urging others to do the same.

Second, Neuhaus wisely employed both logical and emotive tactics in his debate. Humans are not merely won over via the power of logic but are persuaded by their feelings and their experiences. Thus

Neuhaus raised the question of whether we are really comfortable with Singer's conclusions—not merely intellectually but viscerally. Singer himself, Neuhaus noted, could not actually follow his own ethic when his mother developed Alzheimer's. "Perhaps it's more difficult than I thought before," Singer had admitted, "because it is different when it is your mother."[13] Neuhaus pointed to this and publicly pondered, "Aren't we a little off-base when a man has to explain away the act of caring for his aging mother?" Common grace, as Neuhaus well knew, still resides in people, and he sought to awaken their *sense* of compassion in addition to defending the *logic* of compassion.

Third, despite the obviously charged title of the debate, Neuhaus refrained from treating Singer with contempt. He investigated Singer's thought prior to the debate, reading extensively from Singer's *Rethinking Life and Death* in order to interact knowledgably rather than attack a straw man. He sought to refute Singer's ideas graciously yet pointedly and not to impugn the man's motives. As Neuhaus said, "[Singer] is an intellectual and a gentleman, and his purpose is to reduce suffering."[14] Both prior to the public debate and in reflection afterwards, Neuhaus continued to focus on the issues being discussed. He was clear that Singer's position was morally horrific but did everything in his power to treat the man with compassion and equity.

Singer, in contrast, responded to Neuhaus with *ad hominem* attacks, accusing him (and the church at large) of abandoning the poor and living a hypocritical life. Neuhaus accepts the charge (in part) but urges Singer to stay focused: "The debate is not about whether Peter Singer is in some respects a nice person, nor is it about whether all Christians live in a manner consistent with the Christian ethic. . . . He is and they don't. The debate is about . . . his advocacy of the morally monstrous."[15]

No single debate can offer the perfect paradigm for how we should defend human life in the United States today. But we applaud Neuhaus on several counts: he spoke his Christian convictions in a public forum and did so graciously, intelligently, and prophetically. He encouraged his listeners to take a long view and to ponder societal good (as opposed to Singer's flimsy ethical reasoning, the dangerous "Why not?"). And he appealed to the heart as well as the mind, knowing that God's image bearers are not mere brains. Much more remains to be said and done in the public square regarding life-and-death issues, but we could do much worse than to follow Neuhaus's lead.

Discussion Questions

1. A non-Christian friend of yours calls you, in tears, having just found out she's pregnant. The father is out of the picture, and she doesn't feel capable—financially or psychologically—to raise the child. She is planning on "getting rid of it." What would be the first words out of your mouth? How would you try to persuade her to keep the baby? What practical help might you give?

2. Consider a scenario in which the nation is debating whether to legalize euthanasia in all fifty states. A local news team is in your neighborhood and asks you for an interview. You have a total of two minutes to respond. What would you say?

Recommended Reading

Beckwith, Francis. *Politically Correct Death: Answering the Arguments for Abortion Rights.* Grand Rapids, MI: Baker, 1993. Probably the best systematic treatment of the pro-life position. Advanced.

George, Robert P., and Christopher Tollefsen. *Embryo: A Defense of Human Life.* New York: Doubleday, 2008. This little book argues that embryos are human beings from the beginning. George is a professor of law at Princeton. Tollefsen is a professor of philosophy at the University of South Carolina. Intermediate.

Klusendorf, Scott. *The Case for Life: Equipping Christians to Engage the Culture.* Wheaton, IL: Crossway, 2009. An excellent one-stop beginner's guide to defending the pro-life position. Beginner-intermediate.

Kreeft, Peter. *The Unaborted Socrates: A Dramatic Debate on the Issues Surrounding Abortion.* Downers Grove, IL: IVP, 1983. Kreeft uses logic and wit to show that the abortion question really revolves around one question: Is an unborn baby a human being? Beginner-intermediate.

Mitchell, C. Ben, and D. Joy Riley, MD. *Christian Bioethics: A Guide for Pastors, Health Care Professionals, and Families.* Nashville, TN: B&H, 2014. An excellent introduction to bioethical issues, including abortion, euthanasia, and physician-assisted suicide. Mitchell is a professor of philosophy at Union University. Riley is board-certified medical doctor specializing in internal medicine. Beginner-intermediate.

Chapter 8

Marriage and Sexuality

Over the course of the past century, debates about marriage and sexuality continue to press to the forefront of American public life. Presidential candidates are grilled regarding their stance on sexuality. Corporations are panned or praised based on the views of their owners. Legal cases regarding sexuality are heard regularly in courts around the country, sometimes rising to the level of the Supreme Court.

In years past debates about sexuality centered on "free love," no-fault divorce, and other manifestations of the so-called sexual revolution. While those issues are still relevant, the public debate has recently focused on one area of sexuality in particular—homosexuality. Years to come will no doubt raise other specific questions, but our task, as a church, is to promote a biblical view of sexuality amid a deeply confused and broken culture.

A Biblical View of Marriage and Sexuality

Both marriage and sexuality appear at the beginning of God's story. We are told that God created humanity "male and female," revealing that gender differentiation is part of the created order (Gen 1:27). Marriage actually forms the pinnacle of the creation story, as God instructs the man and the woman to cleave to each other (Gen 2:23–24) and to "be fruitful and multiply and fill the earth" (Gen 1:28).

Although one might be tempted to skip the Genesis account when examining the biblical teaching about marriage and sexuality, such hastiness would be foolish. The Genesis account stands as the seed of the rich biblical teaching on marriage and sexuality. When Jesus, for instance, was questioned about a specific sexual debate of his day (essentially no-fault divorce), he responded by pointing his interlocutors back to the beginning (Matt 19:3–9). Discussions of sexuality that focus exclusively on biblical *prohibitions* while disregarding the biblical *design* are bound to become muddled and arbitrary.

Paul, too, looks back to the Genesis account to frame the meaning of marriage. He picks up the "cleave" terminology and applies it to the way a man should love his wife—sacrificially and wholeheartedly (Eph 5:28–31). Yet Paul adds a dimension that was only latent in Genesis. He points out that the covenant we express in marriage is meant to act as a reflection of God's commitment to reconcile sinners to himself through Jesus Christ. In short, marriage points to the gospel (Eph 5:32). This helps show why Scripture finds a broken marriage covenant so tragic: when the marriage covenant is broken, it tells the world a lie about God's love toward us—that it is conditional, fragile, and unreliable.

Many contemporary critics accuse Christians of having a diminished, even stunted, appreciation of sex. The biblical picture, however, reveals that God created sex and enjoins us to enjoy it as his good gift within the boundaries he has given. Within the marriage covenant husband and wife are encouraged to delight in each other sexually. Proverbs, for instance, instructs a husband to "rejoice with the wife of [his] youth" and to "let her breasts satisfy [him] at all times" (Prov 5:18–19 NKJV). And much of the Song of Songs promotes marital sexual delight in vivid ways. Contrary to the predominant culture depiction—in which sex is merely an appetite to satiate—Scripture paints a picture of sex that is lofty and beautiful. Sexual fulfillment is not something God is ashamed of; it is a good gift to humanity that God intended to point back to him.

Homosexuality

Christian sexual ethics have never enjoyed universal societal support. But what offends people varies from culture to culture and from age to age. One of the major points of contention for us today regards homosexuality. Is it wrong for men to have sex with men (or women with women)? If so, why?

The biblical teaching on same-sex practice has, for centuries, been understood to be abundantly clear. In addition to the creational paradigm discussed above—in which marriage is understood as a permanent union between one man and one woman—Scripture addresses homosexual behavior specifically in several places. It is by no means a *frequent* topic, but the verdict is still unambiguous: from Old Testament law (Lev 18:22; 20:13) through to New Testament reflection (Rom 1:24–27; 1 Cor 6:9–11; 1 Tim 1:9–11), homosexual practice is roundly prohibited.

Many proponents of homosexuality attempt to argue that the Bible does not *really* condemn same-sex behavior—not as we understand it today, at least. What the apostle Paul had in mind, for instance, was male prostitution and pedophilia. Committed same-sex relationships did not exist in Paul's day, they say; thus his prohibitions do not apply.[1]

But this interpretation does not make sense of the texts. As historian Thomas Hubbard has amply demonstrated, homosexuality in the ancient world manifested in many forms, including committed, lifelong, same-sex partnerships.[2] Paul could have distinguished between appropriate and inappropriate homosexual behavior, but he opted instead for the blanket prohibition. Those who claim Scripture supports same-sex behavior work hard to make their case. We do not wish to impugn their motives, but we find their biblical interpretations severely wanting, more indebted to modern assumptions than responsible exegesis.

As for extrabiblical evidence, one may note, for instance, that homosexuality runs contrary to biological design: the man and woman's genitals seem to be *made* for each other; the homosexual act, on the other hand, goes against biological design and even damages the male body.[3] Additionally, homosexual behavior is inherently nongenerative. It is sex without any possibility of procreation, intrinsically sterile.

Or we may note the weight of history, which overwhelmingly favors a traditional understanding of marriage as male-female. And as Scott B. Rae notes, "No civilization has ever survived the destruction of the traditional family."[4]

We may also note the inherently flawed line of reasoning that generally accompanies the approval of same-sex behavior. Homosexual ideology does not exist in a vacuum but is one manifestation of the argument, "If they're adults and it's consensual, then what's the big deal?" As Richard Mouw has aptly noted, this is a naïve rubric for avoiding exploitation: "Our capacity for exploiting, and for being exploited, is a very deep and subtle thing—too deep to be captured by simple-minded formulas about what is agreeable to 'consenting adults.' We are vulnerable creatures who easily become confused and misguided in such matters."[5]

Vulnerable and Confused Creatures

Our culture consistently counsels us to "be true to ourselves." In regards to sexuality, this means those of us who feel same-sex desires must accept them as natural, even key to our identity. To deny those desires expression is inauthentic and repressive. But Christians should recognize the danger in this for two reasons: first, our understanding of our identity should never be wrapped up primarily in sexuality but in our union with Christ; second, it is not safe *for any of us* to allow our sexual urges to define what is right and wrong.

Because we live in a fallen world, our sexual desires are warped and broken. We don't like to admit this, so, as Mouw notes, we disguise our brokenness. Even seemingly basic labels as "gay" and "straight" reveal this self-deception. "Gay" implies a happy life, but the lives of homosexuals—especially in light of HIV/AIDS—are often filled with pain and grief. And "straight" implies normalcy; but this is misleading, too, since we *all* are "bent, crooked, broken."[6]

Some of us will feel the weight of the fall by struggling against same-sex attraction. Others of us will feel it through temptations to sexual infidelity or pornography, alcoholism or anxiety. But these temptations to sin, as painful as they are, must never be assumed to be our "true" self. As Christians, we defy a world that seeks to define us by our passions, whether they *seem* healthy or harmful. Only one passion defines us, and it is the passion of the Son of God. Jesus died for us, the broken, and we draw our identity from his declaration over us at Calvary, not from within our wayward hearts. Now, as redeemed sinners, we have the strength to stand on the solid rock of Christ, resisting whatever temptations we experience, however innate they feel to us.

Same-Sex Marriage

Closely tied to the morality of homosexual behavior in today's society is the fact that the Supreme Court of the United States has ruled that same-sex couples have a right to marry. The primary argument made in favor of such a view is the notion of fairness, which is why same-sex marriage proponents refer to their cause as a "basic human right." Heterosexual couples are allowed to marry; why not homosexual ones?

The "why not" question is notoriously disputed during this present moment in Western history. But as G. K. Chesterton once noted, those who fail to "see the point" behind long-standing mores and definitions should be the *last* ones entrusted to alter them.[7] Marriage has, throughout history, been defined as a union between one man and one woman, not least because this is a complementary relationship that produces children and forms the basis of family. Children are not, admittedly, the *only* purpose of marriage, but the connection is not arbitrary.

Nor is it a light thing to revise the societal definition of marriage. The traditional understanding of marriage found its basis in the created order: it was a sexual union with God-ordained boundaries. But the contemporary desire to bless same-sex marriages lacks this foundation. It is, as R. R. Reno calls it, "a purely affective union for the sake of . . . affective union."[8] Once we decide, legally speaking, that we can marry *anyone* on the sole basis of affection, it is not a question of if, but rather when, we will see legal sanctions for such practices as polygamy and incest.

A Public Interview and a Personal Conversation: Rosaria Butterfield and Ken Smith

During a national conference sponsored by the Ethics and Religious Liberty Commission (ERLC) and attended by the national press, ERLC President Russell D. Moore interviewed Dr. Rosaria Butterfield.[9] Butterfield is a Christian who came to faith out of a lifestyle she describes as lesbian and feminist. Butterfield taught for years in the English Department and Women's Studies Program at Syracuse University, where she was an outspoken advocate for the Lesbian Gay Bisexual Transgender (LGBT) community—until what she calls her "train wreck conversion" to Christ.

Evangelicals, Butterfield began, have a lot to learn from the LGBT community. The gay community prides itself on hospitality and fostering an environment of fellowship and care. What they often miss is that the church is the community God designed to provide the fellowship and care all humans need. "The gospel road into people's lives will be in mercy," she said. "If you step into people's lives with a cup of cold water, no one will disagree with you."

The details of Butterfield's conversion are at once common yet intriguing. The Bible, she said, began to challenge her worldview. She had begun to read it for a research project and quickly found herself "undone" by the book's unity. She read the Bible through dozens of times, each time more profoundly affected by the ideas of universal sin, of free grace, of the way God deals with humanity.

She was helped along in her "research" by a humble, small-church pastor—Ken Smith. Ken and his wife Floy had invited Rosaria to their house for years, offering to help her understand the Bible. They didn't want to spar over biblical texts about homosexuality. They simply wanted to have a conversation, Butterfield recalls, "to show me a window into their journey with Christ." They were practicing, simply and humbly, Christian hospitality and compassion. Over the following months Butterfield would see that this was not a mere show: dozens of people came through their doors. The Smith house was one marked by genuine Christian love.

Pastor Ken, Butterfield underscored, is a remarkable example of an ordinary Christian. He invited her over to dinner, listened to her sympathetically, and prayed for her heart to open to the gospel as they studied the Bible. For her part, she went to dinner to get research for her book. But she found "someone who was as committed to community as I am, as committed to hospitality as I am. . . . Conversations about sexuality and politics did not send him under the chair. I also met someone who did two important things at the first meeting . . . he did not share the gospel with me . . . [and] he did not invite me to church." Pastor Ken wasn't interested in a hit-and-run gospel presentation. This impressed and surprised Butterfield: "Good teachers are people who are in the long haul with you."

Both Butterfield and Smith provide commendable examples for us as we try, like Christ, to respond to the LGBT community "with truth *and* grace" (John 1:14). Smith, for instance, shows us the incredible power of seemingly mundane faithfulness. He was not an expert in sexuality but a pastor whose tools were biblical fidelity, genuine love, and dogged perseverance. And he exemplified an attitude that more of us need to adopt, loving his gay neighbor unconditionally, making clear they did not agree, while still drawing her close as a friend. Our love for others must never be contingent on their agreeing with us.

As for Butterfield, we should learn how critical are the extraverbal aspects of our witness—hospitality, community, compassion, grace. These were virtues she treasured through her association with the LGBT community and ones we desperately need to recover as a church, the *true* community of grace. We also learn from Butterfield that while conversion to Christ is always deeply personal, it is not therefore private. Her conversion story illustrates how God must work on the heart of each individual; but once he begins to work, the heart overflows into all of life.

An Op-Ed Piece: Andrew T. Walker

Butterfield's interview with Moore addresses the need for evangelicals to love the LGBT community. This addresses a public square issue but not necessarily a public policy issue. We thus briefly return to the pressing question, "Should same-sex couples be allowed to marry?" and consider the recent article in Time.com by Andrew T. Walker, director of Policy Studies for the ERLC.[10]

Walker frames his article as a response to an argument in favor of same-sex marriage that had been made recently in *Time* by a Christian, Brandan Robertson. Walker claims Robertson's argument lacks logical cohesion and rides on the back of emotional appeals and caricatures of traditional Christianity. He then considers Robertson's claims, point by point. To those who consider traditional marriage restrictions bigoted and discriminatory, he replies that these restrictions are "grounded in the powers of observation that draw rightful distinctions between different sets of relationships."[11]

To those who wish to keep "theology and politics" separate, Walker points out, rightly, that it is both impossible and unkind to lay aside deeply held convictions in the public square. These convictions must be levied for the common good, as is done, for instance (with societal support), in Christian activism against sex trafficking.

And to those who consider this theological view inherently sectarian (and therefore inappropriate in the political realm), Walker responds: "Marriage leads one outside the walls of the church and into the public square because marriage, by design, reveals a purpose about our being made male and female. Marriage has an innately public purpose by bringing together the two halves of humanity."[12] Christian beliefs, while theological in their origin, must be put to work publicly.

The motivation for Christians, then, is not merely to proclaim the truth but to cultivate a flourishing society. And as Walker points out, those laws can be articulated in terms of the public interest rather than being tied directly to the Bible. The government prohibits theft, for instance, not because of Levitical law but because theft undermines a just civil society.

Walker concludes with a word to young evangelicals, calling them not to cave to the prevailing cultural pressure. The traditional view of marriage is not only true to God's design but vital to the public good. If we truly love our neighbor and desire a flourishing society, then we will examine Scripture, respect the Christian tradition, and seek to make arguments based on ideas, not rhetorical flourishes.

Walker's piece provides a helpful complement to Butterfield and Smith. He takes his opponent's ideas seriously, yet speaks directly and firmly to what he sees as a poor argument. He makes use of both thick reasoning (in his defense of the biblical view) and thin reasoning (by referring to laws against theft and the Christian movement against sex trafficking). And, like Butterfield, he calls us all to the virtue of courage in the public square. It takes great courage to challenge the prevailing moral views of the day, as Walker does. It takes great courage to change allegiances as publicly as did Butterfield. May God grant that courage to us all.

Discussion Questions

1. A couple in your church reveals to you that their daughter has "come out of the closet." Confidentially, they mention that they are struggling to believe the biblical teaching that homosexual activity is sinful. How would you respond?

2. The local newspaper prints a "counterpoints" series each week, in which a disputed social issue is debated by two citizens. This week the question is, "Should Christians support homosexual marriage as a civil right even if they consider homosexual practice a sin?" You are asked to write your position on the issue and are given four paragraphs. What would you write?

Recommended Reading

Butterfield, Rosaria. *The Secret Thoughts of an Unlikely Convert: An English Professor's Journey into Christian Faith,* exp. ed. Pittsburgh, PA: Crown & Covenant, 2014. Lively and well-written testimony of a tenured English professor, self-described as feminist and actively homosexual, who found Christ mid-career and left her former lifestyle to marry a pastor. Beginner-intermediate.

DeYoung, Kevin. *What Does the Bible Really Teach About Homosexuality?* Wheaton, IL: Crossway, 2015. In this brief and accessible book, DeYoung builds a concise theology of sexuality and homosexuality before responding to popular objections. Beginner.

Gergis, Sherif, Ryan T. Anderson, and Robert P. George. *What Is Marriage? Man and Woman: A Defense.* Jackson, TN: Encounter,

2012. A brief and brilliant defense of the traditional view of marriage. Intermediate.

Heimbach, Daniel R. *True Sexual Morality: Recovering Biblical Standards for a Culture in Crisis.* Wheaton, IL: Crossway, 2004. A comprehensive introduction to the biblical view of sexuality. Intermediate-advanced.

Heimbach, Daniel. *Why Not Same-Sex Marriage: A Manual for Defending Marriage Against Radical Reconstruction.* Sisters, OR: Trusted Books, 2014. A comprehensive defense of the traditional view of marriage. Intermediate.

Keller, Timothy, and Kathy Keller. *The Meaning of Marriage.* New York: Riverhead, 2013. A compelling treatment of the biblical view of marriage. Intermediate.

Walker, Andrew, and Eric Teetsel. *Marriage Is: How Marriage Transforms Society and Cultivates Human Flourishing.* Nashville: B&H, 2015. A compelling case for the biblical view of marriage. Intermediate.

Yuan, Christopher, and Angela Yuan. *Out of a Far Country: A Gay Son's Journey to God. A Broken Mother's Search for Hope.* Colorado Springs, CO: WaterBrook, 2011. The testimony of a gay man's conversion to Christ and out of his gay lifestyle. Cowritten with his mother. Beginner-intermediate.

Chapter 9

Economics and Wealth

If Christians feel uncomfortable engaging in the public square, perhaps the most acute feelings of discomfort accompany the area of economics. We are familiar with Scripture's warnings, for instance, against the dangers of wealth or against the temptations of greed and envy. Yet we also know that money is indispensable in our daily lives. Unsure of how to reconcile their biblical convictions with the complicated economic world around them, many Christians resign themselves to compartmentalization.

Thus, in our confusion we allow economics to pass under the radar of Christian reflection. All that matters regarding wealth, we assume, is that we give some of it back to God. But this assumption is foolish and shortsighted. It is foolish because economics, as with every other sphere of life, belongs to God. And it is shortsighted because economics affects us all. Economics concerns not just cash flow but, more important, the way we organize our society, the value we place on certain people, and whether we will cultivate human flourishing or suppress it. We ignore it at our own peril.

A Biblical View of Economics and Wealth

God created a world of abundance and placed humanity in the midst of it to flourish amid that abundance. Yet Adam and Eve had work to do: God told them to "till the soil" (Gen 2:15 RSV) and "have dominion" (Gen 1:26) bringing out the hidden potentials of God's abundant creation. They were, in a sense, born rich but still expected to work hard. We must recall that the creative and managerial tasks God gave our first parents existed before the fall. The garden of Eden had an abundance of wealth but not a drop of wealth-related sin—no greed, no theft, no envy.

All of that changed in the aftermath of the fall as Adam and Eve's creative capacities became corrupted. Suddenly wealth was not an arena of endless promise, a field to be cultivated from abundance to abundance. Instead, wealth became an occasion for sin. Scripture depicts humanity's penchant for wealth-related sin in three ways: through our *acquisition* of wealth, our *use* of wealth, and our *love* of wealth.

The illicit *acquisition* of wealth lies at the heart of the fall itself. Given one prohibition, Adam and Eve insisted on acquiring what was forbidden to them. They wanted the forbidden fruit because they wanted to possess knowledge like God (Gen 3:1–6). The result was a cosmic robbery. Thus the original sin of humanity was as much a sin of theft as it was of rebellion. And Adam and Eve's descendants inherited their disease. God's judgment on illicit acquisition is clear: "You shall not steal" (Exod 20:15)—that is, taking something which you have not earned. Not only that, "You shall not covet" (Exod 20:17)—that is, not even *desiring* to take it. The wise man neither steals nor longs to steal but works with integrity for his daily bread and lives in contentment (Prov 6:6–11; 30:7–9).

People also sin in their *use* of wealth. As James teaches us, our hearts are inclined to pursue riches for the wrong reasons, in order to "spend [them] on [our] passions" (Jas 4:3). We are all naturally inclined to close our fingers tightly around the wealth in our possession, using it for our own benefit and not for the benefit of others. But generosity, particularly toward the poor, is copiously commended in Scripture, especially in light of the great generosity of God toward us (Deut 8:18; Prov 11:24; 19:17; Acts 2:44–45; 20:35; 2 Corinthians 8–9; 1 Tim 6:17–19; et al.). What we do with our wealth reveals the true trajectory of our hearts, whether toward God or toward idols.

Both our sin regarding the *acquisition* and the *use* of wealth, though, point deeper to the fundamental problem we have with wealth—an inordinate *love* of wealth. We elevate wealth to the status of lord and savior, which, ironically enough, sours our enjoyment of it. When wealth acts as our lord, we will do anything to acquire it, trampling loved ones and flouting God's laws. When wealth acts as our savior, we are loathe to share it because every lost dollar detracts from our true security in life. But as is always the case with idolatry, wealth makes a worthy servant but a harsh master. The love of wealth is not a path to happiness but a path to destruction (1 Tim 6:10), which is why Scripture warns so fervently against making earthly treasures into idols (Eccl 5:10; Matt 6:19–24). The truly rich life is not one consisting of an abundance of goods but one that is rich toward God (Luke 12:13–21).

If we are confused regarding wealth, we are often equally confused regarding poverty. Because we (wrongly) think of wealth solely in material terms, we are inclined to conceive of poverty in material terms, too. But this ignores the pervasive scope of the fall, which places each and every one of us into a position of poverty. As Brian Fikkert and Steve Corbett point out in their insightful book *When Helping Hurts*, the comprehensive nature of the fall means that every human being suffers from "a poverty of spiritual intimacy, a poverty of being, a poverty of community, and a poverty of stewardship."[1] And until we who have material abundance recognize our shared poverty, any efforts on behalf of the materially poor will only reinforce their plight. Although we the "rich" often try to swoop in to save the "poor" by providing resources, we don't realize that the sting of poverty is much broader than mere lack of resources.[2]

The sting of poverty does not lie exclusively in the lack of financial freedom. It also lies in the accompanying shame, humiliation, fear, voicelessness, and inferiority. Thus the problem of poverty cannot be overcome by supplying material wealth alone. It must be holistic, remedying the deeper deficits created by a poverty of spirit and a poverty of dignity.

Thankfully the biblical story does not end with the fall. God has provided an answer to poverty by entering into our poverty himself. Jesus took on our shame and our humiliation so the poor might be able to say, "God knows my situation, and God cares." He reminded those with material wealth that they, too, must realize their poverty if they hoped to share in his kingdom (Matt 5:3; 19:24). And he graciously provided a way for all of us to stop looking to wealth as our savior. Only when Christ is rightly seated on the throne are we freed to *acquire* wealth with integrity and diligence, to *use* wealth with generosity and wisdom, and to eschew the inordinate *love* of wealth that both divides our communities and destroys our own souls.

From Wealth to Economics: Michael Novak's Defense of Capitalism

One of the great conflicts of the twentieth century (perhaps, in terms of enduring global impact, *the* great conflict of that century) was the long and tense standoff between the world's two superpowers, aptly dubbed the Cold War. The clash at the heart of the Cold War was not merely a result of power interests but a result of conflicting economic systems. Would the world's first communist government in the USSR prove globally dominant, or would the free market capitalism of the West win the day?

On the face of it, the ideological struggle between socialism and capitalism seems difficult to adjudicate based on the biblical evidence.

Scripture speaks amply to the ideas of wealth, riches, wages, work, loans, and taxes. But it does not provide a theory of economics in the contemporary sense; indeed, modern economics has only arisen in the last two and a half centuries. Economics as a system developed in the wake of patently modern developments, specifically the technological advances of the industrial revolution and the (quite related but historically novel) strict division of labor. New technologies forced people to think for the first time in terms of production, consumption, markets, and capital. The science of economics was born.[3]

If applying biblical wisdom to *wealth* was a difficult task, applying that wisdom to *economics* proves even more complicated. Indeed, some Christians have decried the entire approach of economics—socialist as well as capitalist—as essentially atheistic, removing teleology from human action and discouraging categories of virtue.[4] Yet we cannot turn back the clock, and biblical wisdom demands that we do our best to apply biblical principles to the economic systems of our day.

One of the more well-known attempts to do precisely that comes from the pen of Catholic philosopher Michael Novak: *The Spirit of Democratic Capitalism*. Written during the latter stages of the Cold War, Novak's work argues that a healthy democratic capitalist system honors biblical principles more than any other system.[5] When combined with the rule of law and a moral citizenry, Novak posits that economic capitalism provides the best environment for human flourishing—and our best chance of lifting nearly one billion people around the world out of poverty.

Capitalism does not exist in a vacuum. For Novak it is a natural fruit of the Christian worldview, which helps explain why capitalism experiences less friction in societies with a strong Christian tradition. But capitalism is not a system *guaranteed* to lead to human flourishing. This places him in opposition to Adam Smith's notion of the market's benevolent "invisible hand" and opposed to any naïve advocates of an absolutely unrestricted market. As Lesslie Newbigin has wisely pointed out, unrestricted economic growth standing alone is not healthy for a society.

Economic growth requires moral direction lest it become growth for its own sake. And, as Newbigin warns, sheer unrestricted growth is not the same as flourishing: "And that, of course, is an exact account of the phenomenon which, when it occurs in the human body, is called cancer."[6]

Novak, however, still sees capitalism as a key feature in a flourishing society *if* set alongside the other two key components. As Novak argues, a flourishing society must have three interrelated systems: "a democratic polity, an economy based on markets and incentives, and a moral-cultural system which is pluralistic and, in the largest sense, liberal [that is, free]."[7] Or, as Novak would more recently summarize it, "Democratic capitalism, therefore, is a system of three liberties: political liberty, economic liberty, and liberty in religion and conscience."[8] Absent the two buttressing systems, economic capitalism can be a scourge. But if the three work in tandem, tangible good can result.[9]

Some critics of capitalism often point out that the system itself seems to promote vices such as greed and vicious competition. Novak acknowledges that such misappropriations are possible but points out that, when accompanied by just laws and a moral citizenry, the free market encourages *healthy* competition. This competition provides incentive for entrepreneurs, business owners, and employees to build better business models and create better products. And better products in turn provide a variety of benefits to society, both to the rich and to the poor. In contrast, an economic system predicated on socialist principles strips people of incentive to work hard and innovate. The result is not more equity but more poverty.

Other critics of capitalism have pointed out that despite its successes it has not yet produced a perfect society. Such was Karl Marx's utopian critique of capitalism and the great allure of his competing system (now bearing his name). In response to utopian arguments, Novak notes that the biblical narrative reminds us that we live in a time "between the times," a time in which we must respect the realities of living in a fallen world. It is neither possible nor advisable to seek an economic (or political) system that will create heaven on earth. As Novak writes, "Democratic capitalism is neither the Kingdom of God nor without sin. Yet all other known systems of political economy are worse."[10]

Ultimately, Novak supports capitalism because despite its messiness he considers it the best reflection of biblical truth. As he writes:

> Reflect on this a little: Many of the inspirations of the three-fold system of political economy derive from evangelical inspirations such as personal creativity, personal responsibility, freedom, the love for community through association and mutual cooperation, the aim of bettering the condition of every person on earth, the cultivation of the rule of law, respect for the natural rights of others, the preference for persuasion by reason rather than by coercion, and a powerful sense of sin. All these spring from the Bible.[11]

Novak is to be commended for attempting to bring Christian principles to bear on the science of economics. He reminds us that different economic theories lead to drastically different ends and that Christian love ought to motivate us to favor a democratic and free market.

Novak's defense of democratic capitalism further illustrates several features of appropriate public-square engagement. He alternates between thick reasoning (capitalism relies on biblical premises) and thin reasoning (capitalism fosters healthy competition). He exhibits a concern for the good of the entire society, not merely individuals within it. And he refuses to characterize his ideological opponents as villains, though this was rather common during the heated debates of the 1980s.

The Danger of Good Intentions: Jay Wesley Richards on Unintended Consequences

In the United States many Americans perceive that the Democratic Party cares for the poor while the Republican Party does not. This perception exists because the Democratic Party favors a heavier redistribution of wealth, a tendency that those on the left believe helps the poor. But as philosopher and economic theorist Jay Wesley Richards argues, the motivation is a good one but the strategy is unwise and, ultimately, unhelpful for the poor.

In a public lecture delivered in March 2015, Richards sought to encourage his hearers to seek more wisdom in the "art of economics," looking to unintended consequences as well as intended outcomes.[12] "My job today is to convince you of one thing," he began. "But it's one thing that none of us actually want to believe. Simply this: good intentions are not good enough."

Good intentions are, in fact, good. Consider, for instance, the scriptural story of the widow contributing just a few pennies to the temple treasury. Jesus commends her not for the amount of her sacrifice but for the heart of love behind it. Good intentions are praiseworthy. But good intentions combined with wise action are *even better*. Of course, most people understand this conceptually, but, as Richards reminds his hearers, "It's easy to *get*, and very easy to *forget*."

Richards proceeds to argue that good economic intentions often result—unintentionally—in oppression of the poor. Consider, he says, government attempts to regulate rent in urban areas, called "rent control." In the 1970s and '80s, many city councils observed that rent prices were very high in the inner city. In an effort to make housing prices more affordable for lower-income renters, they decided to cap what landlords could charge for rent in the city. Their motive was good: to keep housing affordable for people with lower income.

The consequence of this high-minded public policy, however, was precisely the opposite of what its crafters intended. Instead of making housing affordable for the poor, it created a massive shortage in low-income housing. How? It all hinges, Richards notes, on the landlords.

Think about the (again, well-intentioned) regulations from the perspective of the landlords. They need not be greedy money mongers to have their actions adversely influenced by rent control. Consider a landlord who, for example, had an apartment building with ten units— small, one-bedroom apartments, precisely the sort of housing necessary for someone with low income. Each unit costs $1,000 to maintain, but now the city has given a $500 ceiling on rent. Now it is a fairly reliable rule that landlords are averse to losing money. So given an impossible scenario, they have two options: convert the apartments to condos or commercial property (so they are no longer subject to rent control), or stop investing the requisite amount in the property (so that the property becomes a slum). The result is as predictable as it is tragic: fewer and shoddier housing options for the poor.

Richards closed the lecture by encouraging the audience to discipline themselves in "the art of economics," investigating the unintended consequences of economic policies. We should ask ourselves what he calls the "trillion dollar question: *What will happen next?*" What if we raised minimum wage to $20 an hour? What would happen next? What if the government made welfare more difficult to attain? What would happen next? What if the government forgave credit card debt for those under a certain income level? What would happen next? These will not always be simple questions to answer, but they should be necessary. And if we were to ask this one question more consistently, we might save ourselves from the sort of well-intentioned foolishness that hurts the very people we intend to help.

Discussion Questions

1. What are some biblical truths twenty-first century Americans need to account for when voting on public policies relating to the economy?

2. What are some tangible ways Christians can help low-income persons and families without unintentionally harming them?

Recommended Reading

Bradley, Anne, and Art Lindsley, ed. *For the Least of These: A Biblical Answer to Poverty.* Grand Rapids, MI: Zondervan, 2015. This book helps Christians understand how to help people break the chains of poverty. Beginnner-intermediate.

Brand, Chad. *Flourishing Faith: A Baptist Primer on Work, Economics, and Civic Stewardship.* Grand Rapids, MI: Christian's Library Press, 2012. An accessible little primer addressing work, economics, and civic stewardship. Beginner.

Corbett, Steve, and Brian Fikkert. *When Helping Hurts: How to Alleviate Poverty Without Hurting the Poor . . . and Yourself.* Chicago, IL: Moody, 2014. An accessible book that lays a foundation for social ministry and poverty alleviation by defining Jesus' gospel and mission, then applying it to Christian ministry to the poor. Beginner-intermediate.

Novak, Michael. *The Spirit of Democratic Capitalism.* Lanham, MD: Madison, 1991. An examination of capitalism and democracy undergirded by a "theology of democratic capitalism." Advanced.

Richards, Jay W. *Money, Greed, and God: Why Capitalism Is the Solution and Not the Problem.* New York: HarperCollins, 2009. A lively and lucid argument that Christians can and should work from within the free-market economy (rather than viewing it as evil) to help our world flourish. Beginner-intermediate.

Chapter 10

The Environment and Ecological Stewardship

Environmental issues rarely demand the full attention of evangelicals today. But conversations about the environment surface frequently during public debate, particularly during the election cycle. And these conversations have a tendency to polarize just as much as discussions regarding life, death, marriage, and sexuality.

In the midst of this polarized situation, Harvard biologist and secular humanist E. O. Wilson published *Creation Care: An Appeal to Save Life on Earth*, in which he appealed to evangelical Christians for help in the arena of ecological stewardship. Wilson, recognizing that religion and science are two of the most powerful forces in society, passionately pleads with religious leaders to join with secular scientists in their concern for creation.[1] We agree with Wilson: Christians have a deeply biblical reason to care about biological conservation—and to work together with others for the good of our environment.

A Biblical View of the Environment

Christians who dismiss the importance of ecological stewardship can only do so by ignoring the scope of the biblical narrative. The grand drama of Scripture, seen in the major plot movements of creation, fall, redemption, and restoration, concerns not only humanity but all of God's created order.

In *creation* we see God's intimate care for the entire world. He created it, after all, and continually holds it all together, sustaining it by his powerful word (Gen 1:1; Col 1:17; Heb 1:3). What we see around us (and often take for granted) belongs to God, not to us. "The earth is the Lord's and the fullness thereof, the world and those who dwell therein" (Ps 24:1; cf. Job 41:11). Humanity may be the special creation of God, but that in no way diminishes his love for the rest of his creation. He clearly tells us that even the animals of the forest are his and that he providentially cares for them along with the plants and even the soil (Pss 50:10–12; 104:10–14)! The natural world was created good (1 Tim 4:4) and reflects God's glory (Gen 1:31; Ps 19:1). Thus, as biblical scholar Christopher Wright notes, "Our treatment of the earth reflects our attitude to its Maker and the seriousness (or otherwise) with which we take what he has said about it."[2]

God's first recorded command to humanity was a command to take care of his good creation. Man and woman were instructed to subdue (*kabash*) and rule (*radah*) what God had made (Gen 1:26–28). They were to till (*abad*) and care (*shamar*) for creation, managing God's world as loving vice-kings with God (Gen 2:15–24).

In the *fall* not only did humanity fall away from God, but their sin dragged creation down with them. Instead of lovingly stewarding what God had made, Adam and Eve rebelled and sought to rule the world according to their own design (Genesis 3). The mammoth results of this sin were felt throughout creation, as the universal flourishing and mutual interdependence of God's original creation were replaced with the natural world as we now experience it—a world of danger, violence, and death.

But in *redemption* and *restoration,* we see God's plan to liberate the universe from its current bondage (Rom 8:19–23). The renewal of creation is anticipated in both the Old Testament (Isa 65:17) and the New (2 Pet 3:13).[3] And the picture of everlasting perfection Scripture paints for us is not one in which individual souls are whisked away to an ethereal cloud. Instead, what God intends for his final act is a true *restoration*, a situation in which humanity and the created order will live in perfect relation with one another (Isa 11:6–9; Revelation 21–22).

It is helpful here to recall once more what Al Wolters has said: "God does not make junk, and he does not junk what he has made."[4] God cares about his creation and glorifies himself through it, in the "magnificently diverse abundance of the whole biosphere—land, sea, and sky."[5] We must resist the sloppy theology that exempts Christians from responsible ecology. God still values the created order, and he commands us to do the same.

A Ditch on Either Side: Two Errors Regarding Ecology

Ignoring or Dismissing Legitimate Ecological Concerns

People ignore or dismiss ecological concerns for a number of reasons. They may, for instance, simply follow a political party line that downplays the importance of environmental concerns. For many others, it may simply be a matter of immediacy: environmental issues are often difficult to *see* and are seemingly less personally relevant than other more tangible issues like the economy or education.

But perhaps the most prominent factor (in the United States, at least) is economic materialism. Many of us believe the good life is defined by an increasing acquisition of more *stuff.* Thus the environment is not seen as God's creation, something to be governed with wisdom and love. Instead, it is seen as a means to our greedy end, a resource to be exploited.[6]

Taking Legitimate Ecological Concerns in an Illegitimate Direction

On the other hand, it is possible to allow legitimate ecological concerns to flow in an illegitimate direction. For many activists today, this manifests in environmentalism as an alternative system of salvation. The earth is, in a sense, the goddess, and the goal of true religion is to preserve her life. Humanity is often cast as a villain in this narrative since we threaten the goddess at every turn.

This worldview, as Norman Geisler notes, tends quickly toward pantheism, in which everything is "one."[7] The entire world is seen as a living organism, and all species (humans, too) are manifestations of God and are one with another. In short, nature deserves our respect because nature is divine.

This narrative flies in the face of the Christian story. Nature, though awe-inspiring and wondrous, is not divine. Human societies are always tempted to think of the created world as a god, but it remains a creation of the true God. We need not subscribe to oneness to defend true harmony among God's created beings. We can—indeed, must—care for God's creation, but we do so as ambassadors of the King, not as indistinguishable manifestations of some nebulous "one."

A Popular Book: Francis Schaeffer

One Christian who took ecological stewardship seriously in his day was Francis Schaeffer. Schaeffer was an American missionary who lived in Switzerland during the last half of the twentieth century. He and his wife, Edith, are known for starting a retreat center—L'Abri—that ministered to freethinkers, skeptics, and Christians who were experiencing doubts about the Christian faith. Schaeffer was known for arguing that Christianity is the only religion, philosophy, or ideology capable of undergirding the full range of human life, including art, science, commerce, and politics.

Schaeffer was concerned with how seldom evangelicals had allowed their devotion to Christ to shape their ecology. Their approach, he perceived, was no different from many of their secular counterparts. He was equally concerned that those citizens who did express ecological concern often did so by drawing upon pantheistic philosophies. Some Western intellectuals, such as Lynn White, even blamed Christianity for the ecological crisis.[8] In response Schaeffer published *Pollution and the Death of Man*, in which he argued that Christians should care for the earth both as a matter of love for God and his creation and as a prescient witness to modern man.

Schaeffer presents his argument in four moves. First, he demonstrates that pantheism fails to provide a worldview adequate enough to undergird robust creation care. Pantheism positions itself as the answer to ecological evil but lacks the concepts and categories (such as "God" and "moral") to provide a real solution. Because pantheism sees the world as one, moral distinctions between "good" and "evil" dissolve altogether. Schaeffer writes:

> Those who propose the pantheistic answer ignore this
> fact—that far from raising nature to man's height, pantheism must push both man and nature down into a bog.
> Without [moral] categories, there is eventually no reason to
> distinguish bad nature from good nature. Pantheism leaves
> us with the Marquis de Sade's dictum, "What is, is right" in
> morals, and man becomes no more than grass.[9]

Second, Schaeffer takes aim at another inadequate response, that of "poor Christianity." This is Schaeffer's term for pseudo-Christian responses that denigrate the physical and material aspects of life in favor of the immaterial and "heavenly" aspects. This worldview may go by the name of "Christianity" but violates clear biblical teaching regarding the goodness of God's material creation, the inescapably physical nature of the incarnation, and the patently *earthy* vision of God's final restoration.

Third, Schaeffer turns to the solution, based on two doctrines—creation and redemption. The doctrine of creation teaches that the world's great *dignity* is that God created it, and its great *humility* is that it is not God. Additionally, God created humanity in his own image, with a unique dignity and a unique responsibility to care for the created order. "What God has made, I, who am also a creature, must not despise."[10]

The doctrine of redemption reinforces and expands the lessons of the doctrine of creation. God sent his Son to save the world by taking on human flesh, and the salvation he provides is not that of flying off to heaven but of bodily resurrection. Not only that, but God will redeem all of creation, a truth that should lead Christians to treat creation as God intended. As Schaeffer says, "The Christian who believes the Bible should be the man who—with God's help and in the power of the Holy Spirit—is treating nature now in the direction of the way nature will be then."[11]

Fourth and finally, Schaeffer points out that a truly Christian concern for the environment acts as a witness to the world. He borrows a corporate image and calls the church a "pilot plant." When companies plan to build a large factory, they often build a smaller "pilot plant" to ensure that the larger one will work. This plant acts as a vanguard and as a sort of promise of things to come. The church ought to be just such a pilot plant in relation to creation care, practicing ecological stewardship that will show the world, on a small scale, what God will do for the world on a much bigger scale.

Schaeffer concludes that Christians have, sadly, too often failed to be the pilot plant for the world:

> We must confess that we missed our opportunity. We . . .
> have done little to show that in practice we ourselves as
> Christians are not dominated by a technological orientation

in regard either to man or nature. . . . We have missed the opportunity to help man save his earth. Not only that, but in our generation we are losing an evangelistic opportunity because when modern people have a real sensitivity to nature, many of them turn to the pantheistic mentality. They have seen that most Christians simply do not care about nature as such.[12]

Conclusion

The evangelical world could use more voices like Schaeffer's today. His *Pollution and the Death of Man* exemplifies much that we have thus far commended: it applies the lordship of Christ to an issue of contemporary importance; it avoids the danger of short-lived strategies and endorses a longer and broader view of human flourishing; and it employs thick language to bolster its case, showing the non-Christian world that our theology is not a hindrance to responsible ecology but a great blessing.

To faithfully make a positive impact on ecology, we must enact personal changes and listen closely to ecological experts. It is one thing to agree that humanity bears the privilege of exercising loving dominion over the earth; it is quite another to possess the wisdom necessary to know specifically how to exercise that loving dominion. Thus, we encourage Christians in the field of ecology to help us understand issues that are scientifically complex, involve long-range forecasting, and often carry heavy emotional baggage.

Christians should care deeply for God's creation as a matter of wisdom, as a matter of witness, and as a matter of obedience. As a matter of wisdom, humans flourish most when our environment flourishes as well. As a matter of witness, our ecological concern serves as an emphatic statement of the blessed hope that Christ will return one day to renew his good creation. And finally, as a matter of obedience, God still loves his creation; and he calls us to share in that love.

Discussion Questions

1. You have been reading through Schaeffer's *Pollution and the Death of Man* and are finding his argument persuasive. But when you bring it up to one of your friends, he blows it off: "The environment is a *liberal* issue." How would you respond?

2. What should ordinary people do to show that they care for God's creation?

Recommended Reading

Bouma-Prediger, Steven. *For the Beauty of the Earth: A Christian Vision for Creation Care.* Grand Rapids, MI: Baker, 2001. A thought-provoking academic treatment of ecological stewardship. Intermediate.

DeWitt, Calvin B. *Earth-Wise: A Biblical Response to Environmental Issues.* Grand Rapids, MI: FaithAlive, 2005. A concise and accessible treatment of ecological stewardship. Beginner.

Liederbach, Mark, and Seth Bible. *True North: Christ, the Gospel, and Creation Care.* Nashville: B&H, 2012. A concise and accessible book that argues that ecological stewardship is an act of worship, flowing from the gospel and done in humble submission to Christ. Beginner-intermediate.

Schaeffer, Francis, and Udo Middelman. *Pollution and the Death of Man.* Wheaton, IL: Crossway, 2011. This is a slightly updated and expanded version of Schaeffer's book on ecological stewardship, as mentioned in this chapter. The updated version includes Udo Middelman as coauthor. Intermediate.

Chapter 11

Racial Diversity and Race Relations

A s a nation of immigrants, the United States has been shaped by diverse racial identities and by sometimes volatile relations between those races. The Civil War and the civil rights movement stand as but two outward manifestations of our internal struggle as a country. And while we have made great strides regarding racial equality, race relations remain one of the most explosive and divisive issues in the US.

A Biblical View of Race and Ethnicity

The seal of the United States bears the Latin inscription, *e pluribus unum*, "out of the many, one." As often as we have failed to live up to this inscription in our national life, the sentiment behind it reflects a biblical truth: there can and should be unity in the midst of diversity.

God's creational design, in fact, includes and invites unity in diversity. Part of creation's goodness is seen in what Kuyper calls the "infinite diversity" of each creational domain. Even a cursory glance at nature shows us that God delights in an "inexhaustible profusion of variations." Kuyper writes, "Where in God's creation do you encounter life that does not display the unmistakable hallmark of life precisely in the multiplicity of its colors and dimensions, in the capriciousness of its ever-changing forms?"[1]

This infinite diversity extends beyond the nonhuman aspects of creation to his imagers, among whom God distributes diverse appearances, aptitudes, and talents. This multisplendored diversity finds its unity in Christ, who alone holds all things together (Col 1:17). Apart from Christ our differences threaten to lead to chaos as we elevate one race above another. But God's Word helps us see the order and unity that undergirds our communal and cultural life. After all, every human being of every race bears the image of God.

Another way to say this is to point out that unity in diversity is a natural fruit of the doctrine of *creation*. But Scripture shows us that unity in diversity is also a fruit of the doctrine of *redemption*.

Beginning with the promise to bless "all the families of the earth" through Abraham (Gen 12:1–4), we see a subplot in the story of humanity's redemption. God is bringing back and bringing *together* the divergent races that sin has separated. The salvation God promised Abraham was not for his family alone but one that would extend to every family—and, in so doing, would unite them together again.

The church is meant to give a picture of unity in diversity in the midst of a fractured and warring world. When the gospel was preached for the first time after the resurrection, for instance, it was spoken in multiple languages to people from all over the world (Acts 2:1–11). As Paul would later note, the interracial unity within the church signifies to the world the multifaceted wisdom of God (Eph 3:10–11). Consider even Paul's favorite image of the church, the body of Christ. Just as a body is made up of many members, which all contribute to the functioning of the whole, so the church is given diverse gifts, which are all to contribute to the edification of the whole (1 Corinthians 12).

Thus, when our churches do not affirm racial unity and exemplify it when possible within their corporate life, we send a message that is diametrically opposed to the gospel. If we fail to pursue racial unity in and among our churches, we are saying, in effect, "Christ is a tribal deity whose gospel is not powerful enough to transcend racial barriers and whose beauty is not great enough to woo admirers from all races and cultures and teach them to worship together." For this reason we need to pray hard and work hard for a powerful display of Christian unity between believers of all races.[2]

This unity in diversity will be revealed fully and beautifully in the new heavens and the new earth. The apostle John was given a glimpse of this, allowed to peer in to the heavenly court that will one day characterize all of creation, in which there will be Christ worshippers from every tribe, tongue, people, and nation (Rev 5:9). In God's economy his glory is maximized when diverse peoples are united in their praise of him. The God we worship is so profoundly true, so deeply good, and so compellingly beautiful that he will claim for himself worshippers among every type of person on the face of the earth. Race will no longer divide us, and *e pluribus unum* will be fulfilled.

A Letter from Prison: Martin Luther King Jr.

The most famous American exemplar of a biblical view of race relations is Martin Luther King Jr. He is a household name in America, well known for his tireless advocacy for African-American civil rights. Of his many public moments, Americans are most aware of his historic and moving "I Have a Dream" speech, delivered August 28, 1963, before the nationally televised March on Washington. Lesser known but equally significant is his "Letter from Birmingham City Jail."[3]

King was born and raised in Atlanta, ordained into Christian ministry in 1948, and, after getting his PhD in systematic theology, had become the pastor of Dexter Avenue Baptist Church, a historic black Baptist church in Montgomery, Alabama. Shortly after beginning his pastorate, however, Rosa Parks made national news by refusing to surrender her seat on a public bus. Her protest prompted many to join in a growing movement of nonviolent protest. King would soon become one of the leaders of this movement, resigning his pastorate in order to pursue his civil rights leadership full-time.

In April 1963, King was arrested and jailed for participating in civil rights demonstrations. While he was there, eight prominent Alabama pastors published "A Call for Unity," an open letter calling on King to cease his nonviolent protests. "We recognize the natural impatience of people who feel that their hopes are slow in being realized," they wrote. But "a cause should be pressed in the courts . . . and not in the streets."[4] King responded with a letter of his own, prophetically challenging these men by pointing out that these nonviolent protests were both politically allowable and religiously necessary. In short, they had *everything* to do with Christian discipleship.

King begins with a note of appreciation, recognizing that while the eight pastors publicly criticized King, they did so out of compassion, not hatred. But he insisted that his actions were similarly motivated. He could not sit idly by in Atlanta while his brothers and sisters were being persecuted in Birmingham. As he writes, "Injustice anywhere is a threat to justice everywhere."[5]

King then explains his vision of nonviolent campaigns. There are four stages: collecting the facts, negotiating, purifying oneself, and finally, direct action. Birmingham had gone through the first three, and King was ready for action. This was not a mark of impatience but of necessity. King pointed out that Birmingham was the "most thoroughly segregated city in the United States," replete with police brutality, political corruption, and bombings of black homes. He and his fellow campaigners did not come to the decision of direct action lightly.

Yet why is *direct* action even necessary? King answers: "Nonviolent direct action seeks to create such a crisis and establish such creative tension that a community that has constantly refused to negotiate is forced to confront the issue."[6] African-Americans had not made a single gain in civil rights without direct action. Privileged groups don't give up their privilege unless they are pressed on the issue.

This is precisely why King refused to accept the pastors' counsel to exercise patience. A time comes when justice demands impatience:

> I guess it is easy for those who have never felt the stinging darts of segregation to say, "Wait." But when you have seen vicious mobs lynch your mothers and fathers at will and drown our sisters and brothers at whim; when you have seen hate-filled policemen curse, kick, brutalize and even kill your black brothers and sisters with impunity; when you see the vast majority of your twenty million Negro brothers smothering in an airtight cage of poverty in the midst of an affluent society; when you suddenly find your tongue twisted and your speech stammering as you seek to explain to your six-year-old daughter why she can't go to the public amusement park that has just been advertised on television, and see tears welling up in her little eyes when she is told that Funtown is closed to colored children, and see the depressing clouds of inferiority begin to form in her little mental sky, and see her begin to distort her little personality by unconsciously developing a bitterness toward white people . . . then you will understand why we find it difficult to wait. . . . I hope, sirs, you can understand our legitimate and unavoidable impatience.[7]

For King the great injustice of racism, both personal and systemic, compelled him to act.

Like much of King's work, his arguments in the Birmingham Letter cover a breadth of angles. Racism is wrong not only morally but also politically, economically, and sociologically. Throughout his letter he gives examples of each deleterious effect—the reasons action is required. But only, he makes clear, *nonviolent* action. Like the biblical figures

Shadrach, Meshach, and Abednego, like the German Christians who opposed Hitler, King sees himself standing in a long line of obedient nonviolent resisters. And if he is to be labeled an extremist for his actions, he takes solace that he is in good company. As he points out, Jesus was an extremist of love, Paul an extremist of the gospel, Abraham Lincoln an extremist for freedom, and Thomas Jefferson an extremist for equality.

King closes with a plea as a fellow Christian:

> I must honestly reiterate that I have been disappointed with
> the church. I do not say that as one of the negative critics
> who can always find something wrong with the church. I
> say it as a minister of the gospel, who loves the church; who
> was nurtured in its bosom; who has been sustained by its
> spiritual blessings and who will remain true to it as long as
> the cord of life shall lengthen.[8]

Look to the example of the early church, King pleads, and see the example of Christians who had the courage to be agitators, disturbers of the peace for the sake of the gospel. "They were small in number but big in commitment. They were too God-intoxicated to be 'astronomically intimidated.' They brought to an end such ancient evils as infanticide and gladiatorial contest."[9] We have the same hope they had and the same power.

King's letter, unique among the other documents thus far chosen, stands as a testament to how one can bear witness in the public square from a position of disadvantage. As a black man in a prison cell, King lacked a natural platform. And yet he aimed for the public square nonetheless. We are thankful he did.

King shows us what it might look like to disagree publicly—and that with fellow Christians. His letter, though full of conviction and confrontation, exemplifies love. He begins by thanking the pastors and ends by asking for their mercy toward him. And he makes a point not to dismiss them or demonize them, even though he stridently disagreed with them.

His goal was not to win a public debate per se but to pursue reconciliation within the church for the sake of the city and for the sake of the country.

He also demonstrates the ironic balance of respecting the government and simultaneously challenging it. Civil disobedience, he recognized, was not a path to anarchy but the appropriate means by which to effect change. Yet he imposed limits, refusing to let the justice of his cause move him toward violent ends.

Finally, King expresses and exemplifies a Christian virtue ever in short demand: hope. It would have been easy to let the four walls of his jail cell color his temper. But what issued forth from the Birmingham jail was not a bitter missive borne of frustration; it was a prophetic call to believe in and pursue God's beloved community, to embody in deed the words of our Lord's Prayer, "Your kingdom come, your will be done, *on earth as it is in heaven.*"

Leadership of Holistic Ministry: John Perkins

Similar to King, John Perkins is known and admired as much for his life as for his speeches or writings. He was born and raised in Mississippi during the years of World War II. At a young age, he was abandoned by his father, lost his mother to sickness, and lost his brother Clyde in a fatal shooting by a police officer. In his late twenties he moved to California, where he converted to Christianity.

In 1960, he and his wife Vera Mae moved back to Mississippi, where he founded the Voice of Calvary Bible Institute and she founded a day care center that has been nationally recognized. Both husband and wife leveraged the institutions they founded for holistic ministry that included not only teaching the gospel but also ministering to physical needs. The two, they asserted, belong inviolably together.

In 1969, Perkins organized and led the boycott of white-owned stores in Mendenhall, Mississippi. This led to his arrest, and he was sent to Brandon Jail, where he was harassed and beaten by white police officers. If the officers hoped their persecution would stem Perkins's activism, they were sorely mistaken. Once released, Perkins and his wife redoubled their efforts to minister holistically to their community—to both blacks and whites.

Over the course of the next several decades, the Perkinses opened health clinics, housing projects, and thrift stores, all the while teaching the Bible. For a few years they left Mississippi for California, where they founded the Harambee Christian Family Center. Upon their return to Mississippi, Perkins established the John M. Perkins Foundation—a holistic ministry through which he preaches the gospel and does community ministry, primarily to youth—and the Christian Community Development Association, a network of evangelical churches and organizations working in poor urban settings.

Perkins speaks often and publicly about the evils of racism and has written on the topic also, as can be seen in *A Quiet Revolution: The Christian Response to Human Need, A Strategy for Today*. But unlike some of the other case studies in the second half of this book, we highlight Perkins not for a particular text or debate; rather, we wish to highlight the cumulative effect of one man's life.

Perkins holds together two aspects of corporate witness that many today find mutually exclusive—word and deed. Racial reconciliation is to be battled with both timely words and costly deeds, and his life has given ample supply of both. His public actions, particularly, show us a meaningful way to impact long-term change: through nonprofit organizations that contribute to the common good. Perkins shows us a public life that is (wisely) concerned with more than political change.

Perkins's attitude, too, bears emulating. Like all of the activist civil rights leaders, he faced overt hatred and persecution. But he responded to spite with grace, to hate with love. He poured himself out for the marginalized, more concerned with whether he was bringing Christ's love to a community than if he ever received recognition for it. He saw that a life lived for the glory of God and for the sake of reconciliation is its own reward, a work as profound and enduring as any book.

Discussion Questions

1. How many of your close friends are from a different race or ethnicity? If you do have close friends who are racially and ethnically "other," what have you learned from your friendship with them? If you do not have close friends who are "other," what do you think you are missing by not having such friendships?

2. Can you think of any ways in which American society and culture exclude or marginalize a particular race or ethnic group? If so, what are those ways, and how might we counteract this type of exclusion or marginalization?

Recommended Reading

Cleveland, Cristina. *Disunity in Christ: Uncovering the Hidden Forces That Keep Us Apart.* Downers Grove, IL: IVP, 2013. This lucid and lively little book demonstrates the reasons behind racial conflict and division and provides a road map for finding unity amid our diversity. Beginner-intermediate.

Washington, James M., ed. *A Testament of Hope: The Essential Writings and Speeches of Martin Luther King Jr.* New York: HarperOne, 1986. An accessible collection of the essential writings and speeches of MLK, including an explanatory preface for each chapter. Intermediate.

Yancey, George. *Beyond Racial Gridlock: Embracing Mutual Responsibility.* Downers Grove: IVP, 2006. An accessible treatment of how Americans can move beyond the racial gridlock we now experience toward racial healing in Christ. Intermediate.

Chapter 12

Immigrants and Immigration Reform

Every nation has to grapple with questions of immigration, but for some nations those questions cut to the heart of their national identity. In the United States nearly every citizen has immigrant origins. Our self-conception as a country is founded on the idea of opportunity for immigrants, an idea that many outside the United States continue to hold dear. Thus tens of thousands of people eagerly wait in line to move to the US while thousands more risk everything to enter illegally.

The political questions regarding immigration policy are varied and usually complex. Is our immigration process too open? Too closed? Too long? Too short? For those undocumented immigrants already here, should we provide amnesty? Or deport them? And what about their children, who didn't *choose* to cross the border? Answers to these complicated questions must be informed by biblical principles if we are to avoid policies that tend to be excessively naïve, harsh, or both.

A Biblical View of Immigrants

The Bible does not directly answer questions about American immigration reform. But it does provide relevant information regarding immigrants and immigration more broadly. Four principles bear specific mention.

First and foremost, as we have repeatedly emphasized, every human being is created in God's image and likeness (Gen 1:27). And every human being is offered salvation on the same terms, through the blood of Christ (John 3:16). This doctrine cannot be emphasized too often or clearly enough because it is often rejected or ignored in our society's public thinking. Whether the issue is abortion or race relations, immigration or sexuality, our cultural narrative threatens to create distinctions between those who are truly human and those who are subhuman. We resist this with every fiber of our being and trumpet the fact that every human being in our nation bears the image of God and is worthy of the dignity that entails.

Second, as believers, we live under Christ's great command to love our neighbors as ourselves. This command was first given to Israel (Lev 19:18) and reaffirmed by Christ (Luke 10:27). In fact, as was his custom, Jesus expanded the scope, so that "neighbor" included any person in need. To love our neighbors as ourselves is to act justly toward them and to be merciful to them (Mic 6:8). This sort of justice and mercy means not "turning aside" or "oppressing" the foreigner or the stranger (Mal 3:5; Zech 7:10). It means treating them the way we would want to be treated were we in their situation (Matt 7:12). Whatever the specifics of our immigration policy, they should represent the fruit of just and merciful intentions toward our immigrant neighbors.

Third, God expresses a special concern for immigrants, and we should, too. Throughout the Old Testament, God instructed Israel to leave portions of their fields unharvested *intentionally* so the poor and the alien could glean there (Lev 19:10; 23:22; Deut 24:21). As God never tired of reminding Israel, they were to treat the foreigners among them with special compassion because they themselves had been foreigners in the land of Egypt (Exod 22:21; 23:9; Lev 19:34; Deut 10:19). Nor does the New Testament subvert this concern. As Paul teaches us, we believers were all similarly alienated—not from our native land but from God himself (Col 1:21–23). How can we, having once been alienated but now drawn close to God, view others with anything but compassion? And lest we need *more* motivation on this score, Jesus himself reminds us that the way we treat immigrants acts as a true test for whether we know him at all (Matt 25:31–46). When we oppress immigrants, regardless of their legal status, we persecute our Lord.

Fourth, when Christ returns to renew and restore the universe, he will rule over a kingdom that includes worshippers from every tribe, tongue, people, and nation. Our allegiance to God's kingdom *then* should be reflected in our allegiance to that kingdom *now*. We may be American citizens, but we are also aliens in this world, foreigners who belong to another country (1 Pet 2:11; Heb 11:13–16). We must remember that many immigrants will one day be—and in Christ already are—citizens with us in the city of God.

Barrett Duke

One of the most vocal proponents of the humane treatment of immigrants is an evangelical thought leader, Barrett Duke. Duke has spoken on behalf of immigrants in various manners, including television interviews, speeches, and scholarly articles. We turn first to a recent interview, before taking up an article Duke published in a legal journal.

In 2013, journalist Bob Allen of the Associated Baptist Press interviewed Duke regarding his views on immigration policy. Duke shared a passion for immigration reform that would both recognize the need for immigrants to enter the country legally and provide humane penalties for those who have already entered without documentation. Southern Baptists and other evangelicals, he pointed out, should have extra incentive to urge such reforms since many undocumented immigrants have become members of their communities, friends of their families, and members of their churches.

"So, many of them follow that path, and now they are members of our churches," Duke said. "What are we going to do? Are we going to say, 'Now that you've done all that and you've joined our church, it's time to leave?' It's not going to happen."[1]

They're our friends and our neighbors now, and we believe there is a better way to treat them than they are being treated right now. So evangelicals in large measure are now calling for an immigration reform that will treat them with the dignity that they deserve.[2]

Evangelicals know from personal experience, Duke says, the value many immigrants bring to our communities. They are good, hard-working, family-oriented people who contribute to our society—to be welcomed rather than feared.

Toward the end of the interview, Duke sharpens the focus of his comments, making a specific recommendation for immigration policy. Should we grant blanket amnesty to undocumented immigrants? No. But neither should we enforce penalties that are excessively harsh, like mass deportation. Duke makes an analogy with the way our nation treated teenage lawbreakers in the past. There was a time when certain teenagers were executed. We moved away from that, however, giving teens different penalties from adults. The solution was not to give all teens "amnesty," or to continue levying overly harsh punishments, but to create penalties appropriate to their situation.

A middle path, Duke argues, is necessary regarding immigration as well:

That's all we're asking for here—that we recognize that we are in currently an essentially impossible situation given what is required by law, and we're simply saying, "Let's create a different set of penalties for this very complex

situation, so that we can move on and respect the rule of
law, but also respect the dignity of these 11 million people
who are caught themselves in an impossible circumstance."[3]

Duke concludes by challenging us to view the presence of undocumented immigrants not as a *problem* but as an *opportunity* to enact reasonable immigration reform. A middle path is possible, but the window
of opportunity may not remain open forever. The time to act is now.

In a scholarly article in the *Regent Journal of Law & Public Policy*,
Duke makes specific policy suggestions for what that middle path
should look like. Together with coauthor Richard Land, he makes eight
recommendations:[4]

1. *Secure Borders.* The United States must secure its borders, an
   action that has been counseled (and largely ignored) for roughly
   thirty years. If it does not do so, it "invites infinite repetition
   of our dilemma."

2. *Paths to Legal Status.* The United States should provide multiple
   paths to legal status, including paths that lead to citizenship,
   paths that allow a person to stay for awhile and then return
   to their country, and paths that allow them to work here
   indefinitely but retain citizenship in their home countries.
   Immigrants here illegally need not be deported but should have
   to "go to the back of the line" behind those who are already in
   line legally.

3. *Appropriate and Adequate Penalties and Requirements.* Those
   who have come to our country illegally should not simply be
   granted amnesty. While we sympathize with their plight, they
   broke laws in order to immigrate and should be held account-
   able—but in an *appropriate* manner. Penalties might include
   a criminal background check or the requirement to pay back
   taxes for previously undocumented income.

4. *Cut-off Date for Application for Legal Status.* If there is no required cut-off date, many undocumented immigrants might not come forward in a timely manner.

5. *Limits on Chain Migration.* We need to find a way to limit the influx of extended family members.

6. *Incentive for Highly Skilled Immigrants.* We should provide incentives that draw highly skilled immigrants to our nation so we can bolster our long-term economic competitiveness.

7. *Adequate Penalties for Hiring Undocumented Immigrants.* We should penalize businesses—again, appropriately and not cripplingly—for ignoring the legal status of their employees.

8. *A Dependable Worker Verification System.* We need a responsive and up-to-date system that enables an employer to verify quickly an employee's status.

Duke and Land conclude that these recommendations are necessary for building a just immigration policy and urge the American government to step forward to provide leadership for immigration reform.

Duke's public-square interactions are admirable in several ways. We note three.

First, he uses a combination of thick and thin reasoning to make his case. Regarding thick reasoning, in both his interview and his scholarly article, Duke draws explicitly upon Scripture and Christian theology to frame his remarks. This is perhaps unsurprising in an interview with Baptist Press but is more striking in a journal of law. The eight proposals listed, for instance, comprise only the latter third of Duke's article, most of which interacts with the Bible's teaching. Yet Duke also uses thin reasoning, drawing upon the American legal tradition, the history of public policy, and human goodwill to make his case.

Second, Duke seeks to enact change that will be effective both broadly and over the course of generations. He takes a long view, recognizing how many of the solutions of the past applied quick fixes that only served to exacerbate the broader situation.

Third, Duke recommends a public policy that is both *just* (in recognizing that undocumented immigrants have broken a law) and *merciful* (in recommending a penalty that is humane and appropriate to the infraction). If the conversation regarding immigration more frequently sought to hold these two virtues in tension, we would see much more progress. Arguments and disagreements about policy would, no doubt, persist, but much of the vitriol could be removed.

Russell Moore

Russell Moore, a former professor, now serves as president of the Ethics and Religious Liberty Commission (ERLC). His interactions in the public square include national television interviews and debates, op-ed pieces in national newspapers, journal articles, books, and blogs. Two recent op-ed articles give a brief glimpse into his public engagement on the issue of immigration.

"Immigration Reform Is a Moral Imperative"

In this *Wall Street Journal* article, coauthored with Ralph Reed, Moore argues forcefully that the Republican Party, particularly those in the House of Representatives, should act immediately to reform immigration policy.[5] He rebukes Republicans for their shortsighted strategy of nonaction and urges them to find the moral courage to lead on this crucial issue.

He begins by noting that, although some immigrants commit crimes and freeload off the system, "the immigrant community is brimming with hardworking, entrepreneurial, family-oriented men and women who yearn for freedom and aspire to be Americans in the fullest sense."

He continues by urging American citizens to have compassion for immigrants while at the same time respecting the rule of law. "That means no blanket amnesty or guarantee of citizenship. People who entered the country illegally should admit their wrongdoing, pay fines and back taxes, submit to background checks, learn English, and demonstrate their ability to support themselves." This combination of justice and compassion, Moore notes, will lead to an opportunity for immigrants to take their place in line to apply for citizenship.

Despite writing for a nonreligious outlet, Moore does not hide his Christian foundations. He argues that every person—including the immigrant—is made in God's image, possessing an inherent dignity and value. Only beginning with this theological premise, Moore argues, are we able to forge a viable path for immigration reform.

Moore then turns to specifics, proposing that we prioritize certain immigrants—those with job skills, for instance, or the spouses and children of legal immigrants. He also proposes that law-abiding immigrants should not be forced to wait years for their spouses and children to join them here. This is not just a Christian preference but a societal good: "Strong marriages and families help produce better citizens."

As he concludes his article, Moore calls on Congress to act, mixing thick and thin motivations: "The message is clear. Reform is the right thing to do for our economy and needed for a safe and secure border. It is also the smart thing to do for our future and the moral thing to do for the soul of our nation." Moore recognizes that while right, this will hardly be easy; thus he and Reed close by praying for Congress, that they will exercise wisdom and courage for the good of the nation.

"Evangelical Hispanics and the 2016 Vote"

In another *Wall Street Journal* article, titled "Evangelical Hispanics and the 2016 Vote," Moore takes aim at both Republican and Democratic leaders.[6] He challenges Republican congressmen and presidential candidates to treat immigrants like the images of God that they are, working to reform immigration policies even if that offends their constituents. And he challenges Democratic leaders—the president especially—for unilateral actions that are more harmful than helpful.

The Republican leaders are the primary targets of Moore's critiques. He anticipates that they will be tempted either to ignore immigration reform or, even worse, enact policy that is immensely harmful toward immigrants. "The Republican House," he laments, "is so afraid to touch immigration policy that it has taken no action at all, not even to provide an alternative to the Senate's reform attempt or to the president's reckless unilateral action."[7] Republicans have, in essence, conceded that immigrant reform is a Democratic issue and have abandoned the field. Moore sees this as a blunder both morally and strategically.

Morally, he again picks up the *imago Dei* principle, reminding these leaders that all people possess intrinsic worth and dignity. While an influx of immigrants may be challenging, it should never be viewed exclusively as a burden or as a challenge to "our" resources. Strategically, Moore points out that most of the nation's growing evangelical congregations are *full* of first- and second-generation immigrants. To ignore or disparage immigrants ostracizes those in our own churches and allows Democrats to craft immigration policy at their whim.

The Democrats, too, come under fire in Moore's article. We evangelicals may disagree on specifics of immigration policy, Moore acknowledges, but we can agree on what constitutes *poor* policy. For Moore, President Obama's unilateral action certainly qualifies. But so do a whole bevy of Republican "alternatives," which are too often thoughtless and unrealistic. Both sides need to transcend sound bites and propose real solutions:

> Most important is that candidates don't demonize immigrant communities. Yes, let's deport the dangerous and secure the border. Let's debate how to deal with those already here. But let's avoid slogans that use immigrants as a

foil to win votes. From the immigrant communities in this country, we might just have, playing in a crib somewhere, the next Billy Graham. Evangelicals have started to see this. An immigrant brother in the next pew is a person to be respected, a creation of God, not a piñata for politicians. "Born again" comes in Spanish as well as English versions— and so do voters.

Moore stands out on many counts, three of which we will briefly note. First, he takes fire at both parties—Republicans for inaction and Democrats for wrong action. In a cultural climate in which evangelicals are often treated as a voting bloc (usually a Republican one), such trans-party critique is courageous and valuable. It is a sign that our ultimate allegiance is to Christ, not to a party. Second, like Duke, Moore makes policy recommendations that aim to achieve justice (by acknowledging that undocumented immigrants have broken the law) and exemplify mercy (by urging Congress to make humane policies). Third, Moore uses thick reasoning to good effect, drawing upon the *imago Dei* and the atonement to make his case, while also incorporating thin reasoning, showing that many immigration policies will lead to a better social situation.

Conclusion

Evangelicals have both the opportunity and the responsibility to think carefully and biblically about immigration policy. We will come to differing conclusions regarding specific proposals, but if we unite in approaching the issue with justice and mercy, real and positive change is possible. As Duke and Moore have done, let us also follow the Spirit as we confront false ideas with courage, as we pursue a society of justice, and as we treat *all* of our neighbors with hospitality and compassion.

Discussion Questions

1. A church in your area recognizes an opportunity to reach out to a local Latino community, but they know many of the residents there are undocumented. What advice would you give them?

2. In one of the debates leading up to the presidential election, the topic of immigration reform comes up. One candidate passionately recommends amnesty for all undocumented immigrants. The other just as boldly recommends deportation. Both claim that their respective policies represent the "Christian" perspective. If given the chance, what might you say to these two candidates?

Recommended Reading

Carroll, R., and M. Daniel. *Christians at the Border: Immigration, the Church, and the Bible.* Grand Rapids, MI: Baker Academic, 2008. Carroll is a Guatemalan American, arguing that both sides in the contemporary debate have much to learn from each other and from Scripture. Beginner-intermediate.

Payne, J. D. *Strangers Next Door: Immigration, Migration, and Mission.* Downers Grove, IL: InterVarsity, 2012. Payne points out that the church in the United States should view the massive influx of immigrants not as a threat but as a unique opportunity for Christian mission. Intermediate.

Soerens, Matthew, and Jenny Hwang. *Welcoming the Stranger: Justice, Compassion, and Truth in the Immigration Debate.* Downers Grove, IL: InterVarsity, 2009. A comprehensive introduction to immigration issues, balancing biblical exegesis, historical analysis, and pragmatic considerations. Intermediate-advanced.

Chapter 13

War and Peace

Even the most devout lovers of fiction may balk when considering Leo Tolstoy's *War and Peace,* wondering whether it is worth their time to flip through its 1,500 pages. It is truly a mammoth book. But even the most cursory discussions of war reinforce to us that 1,500 pages hardly scratches the surface. How best to pursue peace and understand the role of war are complex and nuanced topics. And for our young American nation, they have played a central role in our history. As American Christians, then, we have a unique responsibility to make our voices heard, to bring the lordship of Christ to bear in the thorny and messy matters of war.

A Biblical View of War and Peace

The Bible's overarching narrative speaks powerfully to the notions of war and peace. At the time of creation, God's world was marked by peace. The Hebrew word for this is *shalom* and carries quite a bit more freight than the English word *peace.* In English, *peace* generally implies the absence of conflict. But in Hebrew, *shalom* signifies something more: universal flourishing, delight, order, justice—and yes, the absence of conflict.

The *fall* of Adam and Eve broke this *shalom*, leaving us with the world as we now know it, full of strife, murder, and constant warfare. But God would not allow us to languish forever: his provision for a world of broken *shalom* was to send a Redeemer, a Prince of peace, to atone for sin and restore what had been lost. Jesus' redemption and his rule, seen in glimpses now, will one day come in fullness, and *shalom* will be fully and finally realized—the restoration of all things (Revelation 21–22).

Within the broad contours of the biblical narrative, Scripture gives specific principles applicable to war and peace in our fallen world. First, we live in a time "between the times," in which Christ's kingdom has been inaugurated but not fully consummated. This should temper our expectations, as we recognize that we will never reach ideal circumstances prior to Christ's return. As Jesus said, there will continue to be "wars and rumors of wars," but "the end is not yet" (Matt 24:6 NKJV). A day will come when peace has been made perfect, but until then there are often occasions in which we must fight to uphold justice and resist tyranny.

Second, God himself has ordained governments to promote good behavior and to punish wickedness, and he has appointed force as an appropriate tool at their disposal (Rom 13:1–7). Yet governments should only wield their "swords" against real wickedness, not to pursue earthly perfection. They may wage wars but may never wage *unjustified* wars. Scripture points out that many wars (and acts of war) must be condemned. For instance, God judges Edom for waging war without compassion (Amos 1:11) and condemns Ammon for killing noncombatants (v. 13).

Third, as Christians, we should be known as those who always seek what is best for others, who love our enemies, and who pray for peace as a preview of God's promise of a future sinless world in which wars will cease (Isa 2:4; 9:6–7; 11:6). Until that day comes, we must accept that war is sometimes morally necessary. And as a moral necessity, its enforcers are not to be treated as villains but as servants of God. As Israel honored her warriors (2 Sam 23:8–39), we respect and commend those soldiers who serve honorably.

Avoiding Two Idealistic Extremes

No Christian—and for that matter, no "soldier worth his salt" (as General Schwarzkopf put it)—will proclaim himself to be "pro-war." We all desire peace. The trouble is that we have such varied methods for getting there. Those who counsel pacifism and those who advocate for crusades both want peace. Ironically, these two views, which seem like polar opposites, share one key feature: they are idealistic extremes, containing a grain of truth but failing to keep it in balance.

Pacifism: Lay Down Your Sword

On one extreme Christian pacifists refuse to participate in wars of any kind for any reason. They believe that killing, regardless of the circumstance, is inherently wrong. They may use thick reasoning to defend their case, often pointing to the Sermon on the Mount and Jesus' commands to nonresistance there ("Don't resist an evildoer," Matt 5:39 HCSB). Or they may appeal to thin reasoning, pointing out (rightly) that war leads to destruction, death, and often, more war.

We respect those who follow their pacifist convictions consistently, especially those who apply the rest of the Sermon on the Mount so literally. But we maintain that the biblical picture, while categorically mourning death, does not categorically oppose killing. It is wrong to murder but not wrong to execute a convicted felon (Exod 21:12; Rom 13:4), to kill in self-defense (Exod 22:2; Luke 22:36), or to wage war against unjust aggression (Gen 14:13–16; 1 Kings 10:9; Heb 11:33–34).[1] It is, in fact, the *duty* of kings to defend justice with physical force (Ps 144:1). And while we acknowledge that many contemporary instances of capital punishment, self-defense, and war do *not* qualify as justified, these do not invalidate the principle itself.

Crusade: Seek Final Peace by the Sword

It is rare today but historically Christians have periodically adopted a crusade mentality. This ethic treats war as the most effective means for deposing evil. "The crusade," Roland Bainton writes, is "a holy war fought under the auspices of the Church or of some inspired religious leader, not on behalf of justice conceived in terms of life and property, but on behalf of an ideal."[2] Because crusades pursue an ideal, they generally give *carte blanche* to any aggression deemed necessary to achieve their end. What is worse, because their end is ideological perfection, the crusade view turns war into a state that never ends.

We could give many arguments against a crusader war ethic, but here we will limit ourselves to two. First, this ethic confuses our present fallen world with the sinless world God promises he will establish (oddly enough, like pacifism but in a different manifestation). Second, crusaders confuse the role God assigns to his church with the role he assigns the state. As we have argued, there is great wisdom in promoting an appropriate separation of church and state.

Policy Advice to the President: Daniel Heimbach

Just War: The First Gulf War

On August 2, 1990, Saddam Hussein's Iraqi army invaded and claimed to annex Kuwait; and in the days that followed President George H. W. Bush (father of President George W. Bush) took steps to deny Hussein's aggression. Many church leaders urged him not to, employing both pragmatic concerns and theological (pacifist) concerns. In the end Bush decided to act, leading the US into a war that successfully countered Hussein's aggression and liberated Kuwait.

Bush defended his decision using "just war" terminology, in large part mediated to him via an internal memorandum written by a member of his staff, Daniel Heimbach, who serves as our exemplar in this chapter.[3] Heimbach's memo encouraged President Bush to speak with moral clarity and to act with moral conviction, following the principles of just-war theory.[4] Because much of the debate surrounding President Bush's decision regarded the decision to go to war, we include here only the first eight of those principles—those criteria necessary for *becoming engaged* in a just war (*jus ad bellum*).[5]

1. Just Cause. A state must never go to war except when warranted by a just cause. As Bush argued: "Our cause could not be more noble. We seek Iraq's withdrawal from Kuwait—complete, immediate and without condition. . . . We will see that Kuwait once again is free, that the nightmare of Iraq's occupation has ended, and that naked aggression will not be rewarded."[6] The United States was not invading a nation to exploit its people but acting militarily to defend against unjust aggression.

2. Competent Authority. A state must not go to war unless initiated by a competent authority. As a president backed by both Congress and the United Nations, Bush certainly possessed such authority.

3. Comparative Justice. Going to war is not justified unless the cause at stake is more worthy than anything at stake on the other side. Hussein questioned the border between Iraq and Kuwait, but this border had been recognized internationally for years, and Bush therefore believed liberating Kuwait was far more significant than Hussein's border question.

4. Right Intention. Going to war is not justified except with the aim of restoring the tranquility disrupted by the wrong action needing to be corrected. The wrong needing correction in 1991 was Iraqi annexation of Kuwait. Liberating Kuwait restored the tranquility that preceded that wrong action.

5. Last Resort. A state must not go to war unless it first exhausts all realistic nonviolent options. At the time Iraq was offered many diplomatic opportunities to reverse track, refusing them all. As Bush explained, "For over five and a half months, the international community has sought with unprecedented unity to reverse Iraq's brutal and unprovoked aggression against Kuwait."[7]

6. Probability of Success. Going to war is not justified unless there is some reasonable hope of winning. If victory is not possible, why risk lives and resources? In 1991, Bush knew the Gulf War could be won, and he also realized that delaying the war would actually *decrease* his likelihood of winning.

7. Proportionality of Projected Results. Going to war is not justified unless the anticipated results are worth more than the anticipated costs. Keen wisdom is required here as war hawks tend to minimize costs while pacifists tend to maximize them. This was a major debate in 1991, as pundits disagreed over what engagement would cost in terms of lives lost and property destroyed.

8. Right Spirit. A state must never go to war with anything other than a spirit of great regret. Lust for power, glory, glee, or hatred for an enemy all indicate going to war is not justified. Unlike the "right intention" principle, this concerns internal feeling, not external warrant. Bush expressed just such a reticence, when in a letter to Saddam Hussein, he said, "I write . . . not to threaten, but to inform. I do so with no sense of satisfaction."[8]

Just War Revisited?: The Second Gulf War

By the time of the Second Gulf War, Heimbach was serving as a professor of Christian ethics at Southeastern Baptist Theological Seminary. When the United States waged war against Iraq again in 2003, Heimbach addressed the issue in public debate, statements in the press, a national conference, and an essay that would later become a chapter in an academic monograph.[9]

The location of the war had not changed but the justification for it had. When President George W. Bush declared war on Iraq on March 19, 2003, he did so because Hussein's regime would one day threaten us with "weapons of mass murder."[10] The Second Gulf War, then, was a *preventive* war meant to forestall a future threat. Heimbach found this motivation deeply problematic.

A feared threat, Heimbach argued, did not qualify as a just cause for military action. A just cause for war requires that an opposing nation must already be *doing* something evil. "Throughout the history of just war tradition," he said, "the main body of this tradition has always limited just cause to wrong actually inflicted by one state or nation on another."[11] Unless the opposing nation is already launching a strike or reliable intelligence indicates plans for a strike have already been initiated, there is not just cause for war against the opposing country.

Heimbach insisted that just-war proponents must never start treating the existence of "potential future threats" as legitimate grounds for going to war, lest we begin the inevitable road toward crusade. Every aspect of the just-war concept is meant to serve as a restraint against going to war. The threat of what another nation *might* do leads the other direction, justifying war based solely on fear. "If just cause is stretched to allow preventive wars that pursue notions of ideal safety or social order," Heimbach said, "it is no longer a *barrier* to war but becomes an *incentive* for war."[12]

Interestingly, Heimbach points out when President Bush made his argument to invade Iraq, he didn't have to resort to the spurious notion of a "preventive strike" at all. Iraq had failed to comply with their terms of surrender in 1991, meaning that the First Gulf War was, in essence, not over, and could still have been waged under the initial justification.

Though Heimbach offered his critiques of President Bush plainly and publicly, he concluded by saying he was thankful for his president's leadership, even if he had not always expressed himself correctly.

Conclusion

Prior to Christ's return, our world will not cease to be a world rife with conflict. It remains for us as Christians to seek peace, to do what is in our power to limit wars, and to encourage our nation's leaders to exercise force judiciously and reluctantly.

Heimbach is instructive in his engagement with issues of war and peace. It is encouraging, for instance, that as a member of the White House staff, he was able to employ Christian moral convictions to influence the course of history in a significant way. His influence on the elder President Bush employed both thick and thin reasoning, drawing upon his knowledge of just-war theory and how it relates to what the Bible reveals.

Yet even when Heimbach found himself outside the White House setting, he still employed his expertise by respectfully correcting the younger President Bush. Again his reasoning relied on both explicitly Christian ideals and broader social argumentation. In both instances Heimbach had the courage to speak as a contrary voice. For the elder Bush public groundswell resisted military action; for the younger Bush public groundswell encouraged it. Yet Heimbach gave his ethical convictions based on wisdom and justice, not based on political expediency. That he was heeded in one case and not in another is a timely reminder for us, too: while our public words are not guaranteed to find fertile ground, they must still be spoken.

Discussion Questions

1. Suppose that, last week, the national news aired a feature on Christians in the military. Your brother, having seen the program and knowing you are a Christian, calls you to ask for your "stance on war." You only have time for a brief statement. What would you say?

2. Along with military and political experts, you are invited to play the role of "the everyday person" in a nationally televised debate on the role of the US in the contemporary world. The question up for discussion is: When should the United States wage a preventive war? How will you respond? How will you justify the answer you give?

Recommended Reading

Charles, J. Daryl. *Between Pacifism and Jihad: Just War and Christian Tradition.* Downers Grove, IL: InterVarsity Press, 2005. A helpful treatment of just-war theory in relation to Christianity. Written by an evangelical. Intermediate.

Johnson, James Turner. *Just War Tradition and the Restraint of War: A Moral and Historical Inquiry.* Princeton, NJ: Princeton University Press, 1981. Johnson is the world's leading just-war historian, and this book comprehensively explains and analyzes the tradition. The author is not evangelical and often overlooks how the Bible influenced just-war thought, but this book also offers much valuable insight. Advanced.

Thomas, Heath A., Jeremy Evans, and Paul Copan, eds. *Holy War in the Bible: Christian Morality and an Old Testament Problem.* Downers Grove, IL: IVP, 2013. A helpful collection of essays on the topic of holy war in Scripture. Written by respected scholars representing different points of view. Intermediate-advanced.

Walzer, Michael. *Arguing About War.* New Haven, CT: Yale University, 2006. A fascinating book by a widely respected expert on just-war ethics. Walzer is not a Christian but respects Christians. In this book he deals with a number of hard issues (e.g., terrorism, humanitarian intervention) and analyzes several recent wars (e.g., Kosovo, Afghanistan). Intermediate.

Walzer, Michael. *Just and Unjust Wars: A Moral Argument with Historical Illustrations,* 3rd ed. New York: Basic Books, 2000. After a defense of just-war theory, Walzer illustrates it by providing commentary on a number of armed conflicts throughout history. Intermediate.

Conclusion

Speaking the Truth to Power: Learning from Augustine

The year was 410. King Alaric had just led his ruthless band of Visigoths into Rome, sacking the city. For the Romans this devastating event demanded interpretation. What had weakened mighty Rome and brought her to her knees? Why was she *now* being dominated after centuries of being the dominator?

The growing answer in many Roman minds was that Christianity was at fault. The Roman emperor Constantine had adopted Christianity just a century before, acting as both a confirmation of this growing faith and as an enormous catalyst for it. With Constantine's official endorsement Christianity experienced explosive growth, leading to the eventual outlawing of the pagan gods. But many of the intellectual elites in Rome saw this as a dangerous betrayal of Rome's roots, the cause of their present distress. Rome had been beaten to her knees, they argued, because the Romans had forsaken their gods and their founding political narrative.

Roman Christians, concerned for their weakened empire, sought to counter this alarmist pagan narrative. But they found themselves largely insufficient for the task. Such was the case for a prominent Roman official in North Africa. Marcellinus was a Christian who found himself in the corridors of cultural power and who asked Augustine to help him and other Christians refute the pagan narrative.[1]

Augustine was a bishop in the region of Hippo in North Africa and would soon emerge as the most influential theological voice of the next millennium. For Augustine, as for the other Christians throughout the Roman Empire, Alaric's attack demanded explanation. So Augustine reached for his pen and offered up an answer—*City of God.*

Written to defend Christianity during a time when society had begun to decry the faith, *City of God* is particularly timely for Christians living in the twenty-first century United States. Augustine gives us a towering example of what it means to live as Christians for the sake of our beleaguered city, even when—perhaps *especially* when—that city views us with suspicion. We close by noting four ways Augustine's *City of God* can guide us today.

Exposing False Narratives

In the first third of *City of God,* Augustine devotes himself to exposing the deep incoherence of the pagan narrative. In relation to the pagan *gods*, he shows that the Romans never could decide which deities were actually in control and that the preeminent Roman historian of religion, Marcus Varro, didn't really believe in the gods anyway. He surveys the Roman gods, exposing their immorality, injustice, and inability to save the Romans from disaster.

The Roman *political narrative* comes under similar fire. Augustine admires Virgil but notes that the mythical story of Romulus, Remus, and Rome's founding (as told by Virgil) is actually a verdict *against* Rome. The pagan intellectuals viewed justice as the key to their history, but Augustine points to Virgil to say: "From the very beginning, Rome has been founded on a lust for power. Your pretention to justice was always simply a moral smokescreen."

Augustine's decision to attack the Roman system of religion, philosophy, and politics must not be interpreted as a petty lashing out. It was a fierce rejoinder but a calculated one. He sensed the inherent weaknesses of the Roman worldview and sought to "take the roof off" of it, allowing the realities of the external world to beat in upon the Romans as they stood naked and exposed before reality.[2] Thus Augustine spent hundreds of pages revealing the inner inconsistencies and logical problems of the prevailing Roman view so they might be forced to seek ideological shelter elsewhere. They had to perceive the deep inadequacies of the Roman religious, philosophical, and political narrative so they would be existentially prepared to comprehend the adequacy of the biblical narrative. The Romans knew something was wrong when Alaric was at the city gates; Augustine wanted to show them that something had gone wrong—fatally wrong—far earlier.

From Augustine we learn the value of deep cultural exegesis. Augustine was only able to counter the Roman pagan narrative because he knew it intimately—better than most of his opponents. We must do the same, learning to read our cultural and political context if we wish to speak the gospel with prescience and contribute to the common good. And when we recognize that the reigning narrative of our culture leads not toward human flourishing but over a cliff of destruction, we must act in love by exposing the narrative for the lie that it is. The results of a faulty narrative are slow but certain. We dare not wait until Rome is burning to raise the alarm.

Proclaiming the True Story of the World

In the latter portion of *City of God*, Augustine traces the biblical narrative of creation, fall, and redemption, arguing that this narrative explains the world better than the pagan Roman narrative.[3] The biblical narrative, he says, simply has more explanatory power: it alone makes sense of the world. After systematically answering every challenge from *within* the Roman worldview, Augustine turns to the Bible to provide new questions, new categories, an entirely new framework. He has finished cross-examining his opponent's witnesses and now clears his throat to make his own defense.

At the center of Augustine's strategy is his "Two City" argument. For Augustine all of human society can be divided into two cities—the City of Man and the City of God. The two cities take center stage early on in the biblical narrative when Cain murders Abel. They provide the dramatic tension throughout the rest of Scripture. And they persist, Augustine argues, to the present day. On one side are the citizens of the City of Man, defined by the love of temporal things, ruled by idolatrous passions, and headed for ultimate destruction. On the other side are citizens of the City of God, defined by the love of an eternal kingdom, ruled by Christ, and headed toward eternal life.

Augustine wants to make abundantly clear that Christ and his church are not "part of" any other larger narrative. They are not actors on the stage of a grand Roman drama—not even the chief actors. The truth of the matter is exactly the opposite: Rome herself is only a minor character in the grand sweep of the history of Christ and his people. All of history centers on Christ and his people, rather than on Rome and her people. Despite all her grand conceptions of her worth, Rome was never as mighty as she believed. Her rise to power, her centuries of dominance, her precipitous downfall—all these were but peripheral scenes in a much greater story. Augustine invites his readers to believe in Christ, to follow the one who actually stands at the center of the greatest story ever told.

Augustine teaches us the significance of the Bible's master narrative for our public-square interactions. The biblical narrative frames reality, which as we have argued throughout this book, puts all other stories in proper perspective. As Craig Bartholomew and Michael Goheen write, "If we really want to recover the authority of Scripture in our lives, then we urgently need to recover the Bible as a grand story that tells us of God's ways with the world from creation to re-creation, from the garden of Eden to the new Jerusalem. Only thus will we see our way clear to indwell God's story and relate it to all of life today."[4]

Recognizing the Public Nature of Christianity

At the age of eighteen, Augustine discovered the writings of Cicero, which awakened in him the desire to become a philosopher. It was a winding road, spanning fourteen years and taking him from Manichaean dualism to skepticism, from skepticism to Neoplatonism, and ultimately, from Neoplatonism to Christianity. By the end of it, Augustine had read widely in Greco-Roman philosophy, theology, and history, and was more prepared than most to understand his cultural context and speak to it. In his writings Augustine drew upon Plato and Varro, Cicero and Virgil—easily and with authenticity, whenever he pleased. He employed Roman theological and philosophical vocabulary whenever it served his primary strategy of promoting Christ's kingship and the common good. Having been a sincere pagan philosopher for years, he was fair-minded to his pagan opponents; he did not, for the most part, create straw men.

But Augustine was also a tireless proponent of the gospel, laboring as a pastor, theologian, apologist, and philosopher. He knew the biblical writings well, having saturated his thought in Scripture so thoroughly that he could show the internal coherence and superior beauty of the biblical story line from a variety of angles. He was always able to answer Rome's most pressing questions within linguistic and conceptual categories familiar to them, but he never stopped there. He also introduced his Roman opponents to special revelation and, in so doing, bequeathed to them a different set of questions, a fuller set of categories to help them understand themselves and the world.

Augustine exemplified a coveted combination that was as rare in his day as it is in ours: he became a master student of both Scripture and his culture.

From Augustine, therefore, we learn the value of being prepared, when the time arises, to speak a timely word for the common good. Such a timely word must be informed not only by serious cultural exegesis but also by religiously informed argumentation. Cultural parlance can carry us only so far; and on certain issues, as we have seen, it can carry us quite a ways. But eventually we must publicly speak and argue as Christians. As we have shown throughout this book, the real question is not *whether* to bring our religious beliefs into politics but how to do so in a helpful rather than a harmful manner. This remains an indispensable question, no matter how difficult it is to answer.

Contrary to the views of its twenty-first-century cultured despisers, Christianity is not a liability to society. Of course, there are those persons who, like the Roman intellectuals of Augustine's day, maintain that Christianity is pernicious. However, we take comfort in the fact that we are not the first generation to receive such scorn for the sake of Christ, and we respond with clarity and grace: Christianity is not a hindrance to public life but a great blessing. When Christians are true to their Lord, they are the salt of the earth, seasoning and preserving their society. We Christians should be, without qualification, the heart and strength of every good social effort. As an anonymous second-century apologist aptly said, "In a word, what the soul is to the body, Christians are to the world."[5]

Choosing Between Thick and Thin Discourse

Throughout our case studies we have seen Christians choose between thick and thin types of discourse. Should we speak with the thick discourse of Christian particularity, relying on Scripture to make our arguments, at the risk of being dismissed or misunderstood? Or should we speak the thin discourse of translation, using language that is less specifically Christian, at the risk of losing some of the distinctiveness of the particular point we are trying to make? Here, once again, Augustine tutors us as we bring Christianity to bear on the public square.

Augustine adapted his strategy depending on where, to whom, and on what he was discoursing. On the one hand, he was not averse to thin discourse as he sometimes made powerful, refined, and nuanced arguments that did not explicitly make use of special revelation. On the other hand, in *City of God* and other writings, he employed powerfully thick discourse as he spoke directly from the Scriptures. In the *communication* of his arguments, Augustine relied on wisdom to determine when to deploy thick or thin language. At times his readers could easily recognize the Christian moorings; at other times those foundations were subtler. We should practice a similar flexibility.

But make no mistake: Augustine's *construction* and *conceptualization* of his views never sidelined special revelation and thick reasoning. He always wrote, thought, and argued *as a Christian*. As James K. A. Smith has argued, Augustine refused to circumscribe God's grace to a "sacred" realm or reduce himself to hoping for a good natural ordering of society.[6] Indeed, Augustine's public theology rested on the bedrock theological framework in which grace restores nature. He recognized that there is only one realm, a realm that includes both nature and grace, both human reason and divine revelation.

Augustine understood Christ's lordship to be as wide as creation and, therefore, as wide as public life. There was no truly secular realm for Augustine, no piece of life unaffected by the lordship of Christ. Every square inch of it belongs to Christ, and every square inch ought to be made to honor him. So whether the question at hand concerns invading Visigoths or suicide-assisting physicians, the death of an empire or the death of an unborn child, the political narrative of Virgil or the political narrative of the United States, the answer must always start at the same place: there is one Creator, one Savior, and one Lord.

Conclusion

There is still one God. And the United States, despite its flaws, is still "one nation under God." That tiny phrase has proven contentious in recent years. For many it signals an arrogant and dangerous patriotism. But as Richard John Neuhaus writes, it should indicate the exact opposite:

> To say that ours is a nation under God is both a statement
> of theological fact and of moral aspiration. As a theological
> cal fact, it is true of all nations. As a moral aspiration, it is
> markedly—although perhaps not singularly—true of the
> United States of America. To say that we are a nation under
> God means, first of all, that we are under Divine judgment.
> It is also a prayer that we may be under Providential care.
> It is not a statement of patriotic pride, although many may
> think it is, but of patriotic humility.[7]

As we seek the good of our nation by faithfully applying Christianity to the public square, we must never forget that we stand under the watchful eye of God. Ours in not a specially chosen and beloved nation, but it is a nation under God. So we pray that the Lord would give us the grace and wisdom necessary to speak faithfully in our era. We pray that our witness may act as a preview of God's kingdom, however temporary and imperfect. And we pray that God would give us the divine combination of humility and boldness only he can provide, so we would never tire in our efforts for our nation.

Modern political prophets will continue to debate whether our nation, in coming years, will experience global ascendance or imminent decline. They will, at times, point their accusing finger toward

Christianity, calling it the scourge of American society. They will wonder aloud if the biblical narrative really has the power to explain the world around us. And as they do, we must, with Augustine, calmly and confidently proclaim the true story of the world. We have seen the final act, and it is good. It is very, very good.

Notes

Introduction

1. Gilbert K. Chesterton, *What's Wrong with the World?* (New York: Dodd, Mead, 1912), 198.

2. James Davison Hunter, *To Change the World: The Irony, Tragedy, and Possibility of Christianity in the Late Modern World* (Oxford: Oxford University Press, 2010), 101–75.

3. Cal Thomas and Ed Dodson, *Blinded by Might: Why the Religious Right Can't Save America* (Grand Rapids, MI: Zondervan, 1999). Also see Richard John Neuhaus's brief reflection on *Blinded by Might*, in which he argues that Thomas and Dodson had put too much hope in the political process, setting themselves up for the eventual deflation of those hopes. Richard John Neuhaus, "The Public Square," *First Things* 94 (June 1999), 66–67.

Chapter 1

1. Richard John Neuhaus, "Putting First Things First," *First Things* 1 (March 1990), 7.

2. Albert M. Wolters, *Creation Regained*, 2nd ed. (Grand Rapids, MI: Eerdmans, 2005), 48–49. Emphasis added.

3. Martin Luther, *Luther's Works* (ed. Jaroslav Pelikan; St. Louis: Concordia, 1955–1986), 25:426.

4. Wolters, *Creation Regained*, 53.

5. The terms *structural* and *directional* are terms contemporary theologians use to describe the tension between good and evil in the various spheres of life. See ibid., 87–114.

6. Al Wolters writes: "Anything in creation can be directed either toward or away from God. This double direction applies not only to individual human beings

143

but also to such cultural phenomena as technology, art, and scholarship, to such societal institutions as labor unions, schools, and corporations, and to such human functions as emotionality, sexuality, and rationality." Wolters, *Creation Regained*, 59.

7. Alfred Lord Tennyson, *In Memoriam A. H. H.*, 1850, Canto 56.

8. John Newton, "Amazing Grace."

9. Lesslie Newbigin, *Signs Amid the Rubble: The Purposes of God in Human History* (Grand Rapids, MI: Eerdmans, 2003), 55. Emphasis added.

Chapter 2

1. For introductions to these competing theological visions, see Al Wolters, *Creation Regained*, 2nd ed. (Grand Rapids, MI: Eerdmans, 2005); or Michael W. Goheen and Craig G. Bartholomew, *Living at the Crossroads* (Grand Rapids, MI: Baker, 2008), 51–66.

2. There is no single set of labels for the two kingdoms. For example, Luther referred to left-handed and right-handed kingdoms. Other proponents speak of a common kingdom and an eschatological kingdom. Yet others refer to a natural kingdom and a spiritual kingdom.

3. Martin Luther, "Sermon on the Mount," in Jaroslav Pelikan, trans., *Luther's Works* 21 (St. Louis: Concordia, 1956), 90.

4. Karl Barth famously argued that the "two kingdoms" theology operative in twentieth-century Germany paved the way for a dangerous social passivism that actually served to strengthen natural paganism instead of restricting it.

5. Abraham Kuyper, "Common Grace," in *Abraham Kuyper: A Centennial Reader* (Grand Rapids, MI: Eerdmans, 1998), 173. Emphasis original.

6. C. S. Lewis, *Christian Reflections* (London: Geoffrey Bles, 1967), 33.

7. Abraham Kuyper, *E Voto Dordraceno. Toelichting op den Heidelbergschen Catechismus*, vol. 4., 465–66. Cited by Timothy P. Palmer, "The Two-Kingdom Doctrine: A Comparative Study," in Steve Bishop and John H. Kok, *On Kuyper* (Sioux City, IA: Dordt, 2013), 147–48.

Chapter 3

1. In recent years this debate has centered on cases in which Christians and Christian organizations seek religious exemption from laws concerning sex, reproduction, and marriage because those laws make them complicit in other people's sinful conduct. For an example of legal rationales given to restrict freedom of religion, see Douglas Nehaime and Reva B. Siegal, "Conscience Wars: Complicity-Based Conscience Claims in Religion and Politics," in *Yale Law Journal* 124 (2015): 100–175.

2. See, for example, Lesslie Newbigin, *Truth to Tell: The Gospel as Public Truth* (Grand Rapids, MI: Eerdmans, 1991); Lesslie Newbigin, *Foolishness to the Greeks:*

The Gospel and Western Culture (Grand Rapids, MI: Eerdmans, 1986). We do want to note that modernity grew out of Christianity, borrowing from Christianity many beliefs, values, and concepts. However, those beliefs, values, and concepts have been moved increasingly farther away from their Christian moorings, rendering them incompatible with Christianity.

3. Newbigin, *Truth to Tell*, 13.

4. For more on the major features of modernity and their impact on Christianity, see David Bosch, *Transforming Mission: Paradigm Shifts in Theology of Mission* (Maryknoll, NY: Orbis Books, 1991), 262–345.

5. Abraham Kuyper, *Lectures on Calvinism* (Grand Rapids, MI: Eerdmans, 1943), 11.

6. For a comprehensive commentary on Kuyper's *Lectures on Calvinism*, see Peter Heslam, *Creating a Christian Worldview: Abraham Kuyper's Lectures on Calvinism* (Grand Rapids, MI: Eerdmans, 1998).

7. Richard J. Mouw, "Some Reflections on Sphere Sovereignty," in *Religion, Pluralism, and Public Life: Abraham Kuyper's Legacy for the Twenty-First Century*, ed. Luis E. Lugo (Grand Rapids, MI: Eerdmans, 2000), 98.

8. Gordon Spykman, "Sphere Sovereignty in Calvin and the Calvinist Tradition," in *Exploring the Heritage of John Calvin*, ed. David E. Holwerda (Grand Rapids, MI: Baker, 1976), 167.

9. James D. Bratt, *Abraham Kuyper: Modern Calvinist, Christian Democrat* (Grand Rapids, MI: Eerdmans, 2013), 132–35.

10. Newbigin, *Truth to Tell*, 59.

Chapter 4

1. For a beginner's introduction, see Bruce Riley Ashford, *Every Square Inch: An Introduction to Cultural Engagement for Christians* (Bellingham, WA: Lexham, 2015). Otherwise, see Abraham Kuyper, *Lectures on Calvinism* (Grand Rapids, MI: Eerdmans, 1943) and Peter Heslam, *Creating a Christian Worldview: Abraham Kuyper's Lectures on Calvinism* (Grand Rapids, MI: Eerdmans, 1998).

2. N. T. Wright, *Surprised by Scripture: Engaging Contemporary Issues* (New York: HarperOne, 2014), 137–38.

3. See David Wells, *God in the Wasteland: The Reality of Truth in a World of Fading Dreams* (Grand Rapids, MI: Eerdmans, 1994) and *Above All Earthly Pow'rs: Christ in a Postmodern World* (Grand Rapids, MI: Eerdmans, 2005).

4. N. T. Wright, "The New Testament and the State," in *Themelios* 16:1 (1990), 11–17.

5. Ibid., 12–13.

6. Ibid., 13.

7. Ibid., 14.

8. Richard Mouw, *Political Evangelism* (Grand Rapids, MI: Eerdmans, 1973), 55.

9. Ibid.

10. Michael Goheen, *A Light to the Nations: The Missional Church and the Biblical Story* (Grand Rapids, MI: Baker Academic, 2011), 75–100.

11. Mouw, *Political Evangelism*, 58.

12. Heslam shows how Kuyper's views on government developed, especially how Kuyper relied on von Gierke for this view of government. Heslam, *Creating a Christian Worldview*, 158.

13. Richard J. Mouw, "Some Reflections on Sphere Sovereignty," in *Religion, Pluralism, and Public Life: Abraham Kuyper's Legacy for the Twenty-First Century* (Grand Rapids, MI: Eerdmans, 2000) 87–109. Cf. Kuyper, *Lectures on Calvinism*, 97.

14. Kuyper, *Lectures on Calvinism*, 96–97.

15. Ibid., 97.

16. Abraham Kuyper, *Guidance for Christian Engagement in Government: A Translation of Abraham Kuyper's Our Program* (Grand Rapids, MI: Christian's Library Press, 2013), 44–45.

17. Rousas John Rushdoony, *The Institutes of Biblical Law* (Nutley, NJ: Craig Press, 1973); *The Roots of Reconstruction* (Vallecito, CA: Ross House, 1991).

18. For an excellent scholarly reflection on the merits of principled pluralism over theocracy and on the need to use reason and persuasion rather than coercion, see John Bolt, *A Free Church, A Holy Nation: Abraham Kuyper's American Public Theology* (Grand Rapids, MI: Eerdmans, 2001), 303–50.

Chapter 5

1. Russell Moore, *Onward: Engaging the Culture Without Losing the Gospel* (Nashville, TN: B&H, 2015), 33–56.

2. Donald Atwell Zoll, *Twentieth Century Political Philosophy* (Englewood Cliffs, NJ: Prentice-Hall, 1974), 94.

3. Richard J. Mouw and Sander Griffioen, *Pluralisms and Horizons: An Essay in Christian Public Philosophy* (Grand Rapids, MI: Eerdmans, 1993), 15–17.

4. Ibid., 13–15.

5. Ibid., 17–18.

6. John Rawls, *A Theory of Justice*, rev. ed. (Cambridge, MA: Belknap Press of Harvard University, 1999).

7. The language of a "naked public square" is Richard John Neuhaus's metaphorical summary of Rawls's position.

8. Richard John Neuhaus, *Naked Public Square: Religion and Democracy in America*, 2nd. ed. (Grand Rapids, MI: Eerdmans, 1984), 139.

9. For a scholarly discussion, see John Bolt, *A Free Church, A Holy Nation: Abraham Kuyper's American Public Theology* (Grand Rapids, MI: Eerdmans, 2001), 303–50.

10. Neuhaus, *The Naked Public Square*, 9.

11. Ibid., ix.

12. Ibid., 9.

13. Richard John Neuhaus, *The Best of "The Public Square"* (Grand Rapids, MI: Eerdmans, 2001), vii.

14. Richard Mouw, *Political Evangelism* (Grand Rapids, MI: Eerdmans, 1973), 99.

15. Mouw and Griffioen, *Pluralisms and Horizons*, 177.

Chapter 6

1. Michael L. Brown, "Jeremiah," in *The Expositor's Bible Commentary: Jeremiah–Ezekiel*, rev. ed., Tremper Longman III and David E. Garland, eds. (Grand Rapids, MI: Zondervan, 2010), 358–60.

2. C. S. Lewis, *Perelandra* (New York: Scribner, 1996), 170.

3. Richard J. Mouw, *Uncommon Decency: Christian Civility in an Uncivil World*, rev. and exp. (Grand Rapids, MI: IVP, 2010).

4. Ibid., 14.

5. Ibid., 44–56.

6. Ibid., 57–65.

7. G. K. Chesterton, *What's Wrong with the World* (New York: Dodd, Mead, and Company, 1912), 165.

8. Clifford Geertz, *The Interpretation of Cultures* (New York: Basic Books, 1973), 3–30.

9. Richard J. Mouw, *He Shines in All That's Fair: Culture and Common Grace* (Grand Rapids, MI: Eerdmans, 2002), 87.

10. Richard Mouw, *Political Evangelism* (Grand Rapids, MI: Eerdmans, 1973), 79–86.

Interlude

1. Richard Mouw, *Uncommon Decency: Christian Civility in an Uncivil World* (Downers Grove, IL: InterVarsity, 1992).

Chapter 7

1. The latter example (Exod 21:22–25) is still preserved—albeit inconsistently—in American law. Those who murder a pregnant woman are charged with

double homicide, indicating an equality of value between the mother and her unborn child.

2. Francis J. Beckwith, *Defending Life: A Moral and Legal Case Against Abortion Choice* (New York: Cambridge University, 2007), 65–92.

3. In the exceptional (but real) instance in which the child's life endangers that of the mother, we consider abortion a *possible* option, though by no means a necessary one. What matters is that doctors and patients recognize they are dealing with two unique human lives. This is not *elective* abortion for the sake of convenience but a question of how to best serve both patients involved. Decisions of wisdom are regularly required in situations like these.

4. These two practices are not to be conflated with a patient's decisions regarding extreme health-care measures, such as using feeding tubes, ventilators, etc. Such decisions, contained in a person's living will, do not actively *end* lives but identify what type of care they will allow in extreme situations. In other words, our commitment to the sanctity of human life does not entail an obligation to use *any* and *all* means that modern medicine provides in order to prolong life. But there remains a categorical difference between opting out of care and actively ending life.

5. Norman Geisler, *Christian Ethics* (Grand Rapids, MI: Baker, 1989), 166–67.

6. Scott B. Rae, *Moral Choices*, 3rd. ed. (Grand Rapids, MI: Zondervan, 2009), 237.

7. Kenneth Chambaere, Robert Vander Stichele, Freddy Mortier, Joachim Cohen, and Luc Deliens, "Recent Trends in Euthanasia and Other End-of-Life Practices in Belgium," *New England Journal of Medicine* 372, no. 12 (2015): 1179–81.

8. Carlos F. Gomez, *Regulating Death: Euthanasia and the Case of the Netherlands* (New York: Free Press, 1991); Martin Beckford, "Fearful Elderly People Carry 'Anti-euthanasia Cards,'" *The Telegraph*, April 21, 2011, accessed April 28, 2015, http://www.telegraph.co.uk/news/health/news/8466996/Fearful-elderly -people-carry-anti-euthanasia-cards.html. I owe this citation to C. Ben Mitchell, PhD, and D. Joy Riley, MD, *Christian Bioethics* (Nashville, TN: B&H, 2014), 97.

9. Richard John Neuhaus, "The First Five Years," *First Things* 3 (March 1995), 67.

10. Peter Singer, "The Sanctity of Life," in *Foreign Policy* (September/October 2005), 40.

11. Peter Singer, *Practical Ethics* (Cambridge: Cambridge University, 1993), 85–87.

12. Peter Singer, "Sanctity of Life or Quality of Life," *Pediatrics* (July 1983), 129. Also, in *Practical Ethics* (New York: Cambridge University, 1979), he argues that membership in the human species is irrelevant to moral status.

13. Michael Specter, "The Dangerous Philosopher," in *The New Yorker* (September 6, 1999).

14. Richard John Neuhaus, "A Curious Encounter with a Philosopher from Nowhere," in *First Things* 120 (February 2002), 78.

15. Richard John Neuhaus, "While We're at It," *First Things* 127 (November 2002), 84.

Chapter 8

1. See, among others, Matthew Vines, *God and the Gay Christian: The Biblical Case in Support of Same-Sex Relationships* (New York: Convergent House, 2014), 21–42, 117–32.

2. Thomas Hubbard, *Homosexuality in Greece and Rome: A Sourcebook of Basic Documents* (Berkeley, CA: University of California Press, 2003).

3. J. Budziszewski, *The Revenge of Conscience: Politics and the Fall of Man* (Dallas: Spence, 1999), 140.

4. Scott B. Rae, *Moral Choices: An Introduction to Ethics*, 3rd ed. (Grand Rapids, MI: Zondervan, 2009), 284.

5. Richard Mouw, *Uncommon Decency: Christian Civility in an Uncivil World* (Downers Grove, IL: InterVarsity Press, 2010), 104.

6. Ibid., 94.

7. G. K. Chesterton, *The Thing: Why I Am a Catholic*, in *The Collected Works of G. K. Chesterton,* Vol. 3 (San Francisco, CA: Ignatius, 1990), 157–64.

8. R. R. Reno, "Letters," in *First Things*, May 2015.

9. "Secret Thoughts of an Unlikely Convert | Rosaria Butterfield and Russell Moore." From the ERLC National Conference, "The Gospel, Homosexuality, and the Future of Marriage," accessed May 28, 2015, https://www.youtube.com /watch?v=cc8wPOHksYs.

10. See http://time.com/author/andrew-t-walker. Accessed May 1, 2015.

11. Ibid.

12. Ibid.

Chapter 9

1. Brian Fikkert and Steve Corbett, *When Helping Hurts: Alleviating Poverty Without Hurting the Poor . . . and Yourself* (Chicago, IL: Moody, 2009), 62.

2. Ibid., 64.

3. Adam Smith is generally credited as the father of modern economics. See his *An Inquiry into the Nature and Causes of the Wealth of Nations* (London: W. Strahan & T. Cadell, 1776). Smith's reflections were so formative that much of the history of economics can best be understood as a story of economists either rallying to Smith's side or declaring him an enemy.

4. Lesslie Newbigin, *Foolishness to the Greeks: The Gospel and Western Culture* (Grand Rapids, MI: Eerdmans, 1986), 106.

5. Michael Novak, *The Spirit of Democratic Capitalism* (Lanham, MD: Madison, 1991).

6. Newbigin, *Foolishness to the Greeks*, 114.

7. Novak, *The Spirit of Democratic Capitalism*, 14.

8. Michael Novak, "The Future of Democratic Capitalism," in *First Things* June/July 2015, 34.

9. In recent years Novak has strengthened his insistence on the moral/religious third of this system. "Although all are required, each generation must discern which of the three is weakest and most needs buttressing. Thirty years ago, it was economic and political liberty." With the collapse of the Soviet Union, however, these two have effectively gained victories. Thus Novak now argues that if capitalism is to be a boon and not a curse, it must retain its moral counterpart: "An economy without beauty, love, human rights, respect for one another, civic friendship, and strong families is not likely long to be loved, or to survive." Novak, "The Future of Democratic Capitalism," 34–36.

10. Novak, *The Spirit of Democratic Capitalism*, 28.

11. Novak, "The Future of Democratic Capitalism," 36.

12. Jay W. Richards, "Why Good Intentions Aren't Enough," a lecture delivered at Southeastern Baptist Theological Seminary, March 13, 2015, accessed May 28, 2015, http://intersectproject.org/?portfolio=jay-richards.

Chapter 10

1. E. O. Wilson, *Creation Care: An Appeal to Save Life on Earth* (New York: W. W. Norton, 2006).

2. Christopher Wright, *The Mission of God* (Downers Grove, IL: IVP, 2006), 398. Von Rad, in commenting on Gen 1:31, makes the point with even more force: "When faith speaks of creation, and in so doing directs its eye toward God, then it can only say that God created the world perfect." Gerhard von Rad, *Genesis*, rev. ed. The Old Testament Library (Philadelphia, PA: Westminster, 1992), 61.

3. The 2 Peter passage also speaks of the present heavens and earth being reserved for a fire on the day of judgment. Although some commentators take Peter to mean that the present universe will be consumed by fire, we believe the fire referred to is a "purifying fire." Richard Bauckham's interpretation is compelling, in which he argues that the purpose of the fire in these verses is not the obliteration but the purging of the *cosmos*. The *cosmos* will be purged of sin and its consequences, including its ecological consequences. Richard J. Bauckham, *2 Peter and Jude*, Word Biblical Commentary 50 (Waco, TX: Word, 1983), 316–22.

4. Albert M. Wolters, *Creation Regained*, 2nd ed. (Grand Rapids, MI: Eerdmans, 2005), 49.

5. Wright, *The Mission of God*, 405.

6. For an expanded response to economic materialists, see Norman Geisler, *Christian Ethics* (Grand Rapids, MI: Baker, 1989), 294–98.

7. Ibid., 298–302.

8. Lynn White, "The Historical Roots of Our Ecological Crisis," *Science* 10 (March 1967), 1,203–7. A concise evangelical response to White's contention can be found in Bruce Riley Ashford, "Creation Care Founded on the Biblical Narrative," accessed May 20, 2015, http://theoecologyjournal.com/wp-content /uploads/2012/01/AshfordR%202.pdf.

9. Francis Schaeffer, *Pollution and the Death of Man* (Wheaton, IL: Tyndale, 1970), 33.

10. Ibid., 61.

11. Ibid., 68–69.

12. Ibid., 85.

Chapter 11

1. Abraham Kuyper, "Uniformity: The Curse of Modern Life," in *Abraham Kuyper: A Centennial Reader*, ed. James D. Bratt (Grand Rapids, MI: Eerdmans, 1998), 34. Unfortunately, Kuyper's view of racial diversity was not consistent with his high praise for other types of creational diversity; Kuyper's life and writings reveal some racist thoughts and opinions. For example, in a speech he gave at the turn of the century, "The Crisis in South Africa," he spoke of the value of racial sep- arateness. Even sympathetic scholars recognize that his writings sometimes give evi- dence of cultural chauvinism or racism. Abraham Kuyper, *De Crisis in Zuid-Afrika* (Amsterdam: Höveker & Wormser, 1900); Kobus Smit, "Kuyper and Afrikaner Theology," *RES Theological Forum* 16:2 (June 1988), 25.

2. Context and geography make certain kinds of racial diversity impractical, even impossible. We should judge charitably those churches in areas of the world that are predominantly composed of one race and one culture. No church, prior to Christ's return, will look just like heaven. This is a goal to pursue, not a benchmark by which to denigrate others.

3. James M. Washington, ed. "A Letter from Birmingham City Jail," in *A Testament of Hope: The Essential Writings and Speeches of Martin Luther King, Jr.* (New York: HarperOne, 1986), 289–302.

4. "Statement by Alabama Clergymen," published by Bishop C. C. J. Carpenter, Bishop Joseph A. Durick, Rabbi Hilton L. Grafman, Bishop Paul Hardin, Bishop Nolan B. Harmon, the Reverend George M. Murray, the Reverend Edward V. Ramage, and the Reverend Earl Stallings, *Birmingham News*, April 12, 1963.

5. King, "A Letter from Birmingham City Jail," 290.

6. Ibid., 291.

7. Ibid., 292–93.

8. Ibid., 298.

9. Ibid., 300.

Chapter 12

1. Bob Allen, "Immigration Reform Becoming Personal, SBC Leader Says," accessed at www.baptiststandard.com.

2. Ibid.

3. Ibid.

4. Barrett Duke and Richard Land, "Just Immigration Reform: Foundational Principles," in *Regent Journal of Law & Public Policy* 3:1, 67–94.

5. Ralph Reed and Russell Moore, "Immigration Reform Is a Moral Imperative, in *The Wall Street Journal* (March 30, 2014), accessed May 9, 2015, http://www.wsj.com/articles/SB10001424052702304185104579437203436109732?mg=id-wsj.

6. Russell Moore, "Evangelical Hispanics and the 2016 Vote," in *The Wall Street Journal* (May 7, 2015), accessed May 8, 2015, http://www.wsj.com/articles/evangelical-hispanics-and-the-2016-vote-1431040230?mg=id-wsj&mg=id-wsj.

7. Ibid.

Chapter 13

1. Norman Geisler, *Christian Ethics: Options and Issues* (Grand Rapids, MI: Baker, 1989), 229–30.

2. Roland H. Bainton, *Christian Attitudes Toward War and Peace: A Historical Survey and Critical Re-evaluation* (Nashville, TN: Abingdon Press, 1960), 14.

3. Daniel R. Heimbach, "The Bush Just War Doctrine: Genesis and Application of the President's Moral Leadership in the Persian Gulf War," chapter 17 in *From Cold War to New World Order: The Foreign Policy of George H. W. Bush*, ed. Meena Bose and Rosanna Perotti (Westport, CT: Greenwood, 2002), 441–64.

4. A detailed description of the rationale is found in Heimbach, "The Bush Just War Doctrine," 446–54; a May 27, 1997 letter from President Bush to Daniel Heimbach confirms the account. Bush wrote, "Dear Dan, I read every word of *The Bush Just War Doctrine*. Truly it is an outstanding paper; and it accurately states my feelings. . . . Many thanks for setting the record straight."

5. Heimbach also discussed seven more principles for the equally tricky challenge of proper conduct *within* a just war (*jus in bello*), including the proportionate use of force, avoidance of evil means, and proper discrimination between combatants and noncombatants.

6. George H. W. Bush, "Remarks by the President in Address to the National Religious Broadcaster's Convention" (Washington, DC: White House, Office of the Press Secretary Press Release, January 28, 1991, unpublished), 2.

7. George H. W. Bush, "Text of Letter and Report from the President to the Speaker of the House of Representatives and the President Pro Tempore of the Senate Pursuant to Section 2(B) of Public Law 102-1" (Washington, DC: White House, Office of the Press Secretary Press Release, January 16, 1991, unpublished), 1.

8. George H. W. Bush, "Letter to Iraqi President Saddam Hussein," reproduced in *Dispatch* (Washington, DC: U.S. Department of State, Bureau of Public Affairs, January 14, 1991).

9. Daniel R. Heimbach, "Distinguishing Just War from Crusade: Is Regime Change a Just Cause for Just War?," in Richard S. Hess and Elmer A. Martens, eds., *War in the Bible and Terrorism in the Twenty-First Century*, Bulletin for Biblical Research Supplement 2 (Winona Lake, IN: Eisenbrauns, 2008), 79–92.

10. George W. Bush, "Speech Announcing War with Iraq," delivered March 19, 2003; text issued by the White House on March 19, 2003.

11. Heimbach, "Distinguishing Just War from Crusade," 84. A preventive war is not the same thing as a preemptive strike. A preventive war is waged to forestall a future threat posed by a nation that is not currently attacking. A preemptive strike, on the other hand, is when a country strikes first because they are certain an attack is imminent. A *preventive* war is not acceptable, in our opinion, but a *preemptive* strike is.

12. Heimbach, "Distinguishing Just War from Crusade," 86.

Conclusion

1. Vernon J. Bourke, "Introduction," in Augustine, *City of God*, abridged ed. (New York: Image, 1958), 8.

2. Francis Schaeffer is known for employing the phrase "take the roof off" in order to describe his apologetic strategy of uncovering the inadequacy of false religions and worldviews.

3. Curtis Chang, *Engaging Unbelief: A Captivating Strategy from Augustine and Aquinas* (Eugene, OR: Wipf & Stock, 2007), 66–93.

4. Craig Bartholomew and Michael Goheen, "Story and Biblical Theology," in *Out of Egypt: Biblical Theology and Biblical Interpretation*, in Scripture and Hermeneutics Series, vol. 5, ed. Craig Bartholomew, Mary Healy, Karl Möller, and Robin Parry (Grand Rapids, MI: Zondervan, 2004), 144.

5. "The Relation of Christians to the World," *Epistle to Diognetus*, chapter 6.

6. James K. A. Smith, "Reforming Public Theology: Two Kingdoms, or Two Cities?" in *Calvin Theological Journal* 47 (2012): 122–37.

7. Richard John Neuhaus, "Political Blasphemy," in *First Things* (October 2002), 92.

Name and Subject Index

Scripture Index